The Lakeside Classics

Historical Introduction

J. W. SPENCER

GAYFORD, *Photographer.*

The Lakeside Classics

The Early Day of Rock Island and Davenport

The Narratives of

J. W. SPENCER

AND J. M. D. BURROWS

EDITED BY

MILO MILTON QUAIFE

SECRETARY OF
THE BURTON HISTORICAL COLLECTION

CHICAGO

The Lakeside Press

R. R. DONNELLEY & SONS CO.

Christmas, 1942

Publisher's Preface

IN times of war it is difficult to determine how many and which of our habitual indulgences should be sacrificed on the altar of patriotism. As one grows older, habits become more and more fixed, and the habit of sending each year another volume of The Lakeside Classics to the friends and patrons of The Press has become so firmly established as part of the year's operation that the Management is loath to give it up.

Fortunately, Congress in its omniscience eliminated books from its price control bill, inferring that the printing of books is privileged. At least such is the interpretation of the Publishers, who have decided to maintain the continuity of the series by issuing this, its fortieth volume.

For the subject matter we have returned to the early days of Illinois and Iowa and are reprinting the reminiscences of two early settlers, Messrs. J. W. Spencer and J. N. D. Burroughs. Spencer migrated in 1820 from Vermont to that part of Illinois of which Rock Island is the center. More than half his narrative concerns the Blackhawk War in which he served, part of the time as First Lieutenant of the Rock Island Rangers. It tells the story of the war from the viewpoint of the white settler and supplements Blackhawk's autobiography which was published in this series in 1916.

Burroughs moved from Cincinnati to Davenport in 1839 when Davenport was a small village. Like all other pioneers, he bought land and started farming, but he soon shifted to merchandising. From his cousin, who was a member of a firm of wholesale grocers in Cincinnati, he obtained on credit a small stock of goods and opened a store in Davenport. He showed business ability, and the store was an immediate success.

His narrative introduces a new character into this series, a pioneer merchant, and his story of trading with the settlers for over twenty years pictures the important role a merchant-trader played in pioneer life, not only making available to the farmers their necessities in the line of "store goods," but at the same time opening for them a ready market for their products. It also pictures the complications and disasters of the use of the common currency of the time— wildcat money.

We hope that these reminiscences of Spencer and Burroughs during their pioneer days

Publisher's Preface

in Illinois and Iowa will give our friends and patrons during the Christmas holiday season a little respite from the war news so prolixly amplified by reporters, correspondents and radio commentators.

We remain,

Respectfully yours,

Christmas 1942   THE PUBLISHERS.

Contents

xi

The Early Day of Rock Island
and Davenport

Historical Introduction

I F another Columbus were to visit North America and survey the entire Continent in search of a promising site for a colony there would be no cause for surprise if his choice should fall upon the entrancing locality at the mouth of Rock River, where the cities of Moline, Rock Island, and Davenport now cluster. From this center, for hundreds of miles in every direction stretches an agricultural Eden. Here is the heart of Cornland, before whose annual output of wealth the produce of the storied Nile pales to insignificance. Here, too, is an industrial development the equal of any in the world. The Tri-Cities themselves are hives of industry, from whose factories the machinery of both war and peace stream endlessly; while within easy reach by rail and highway lie many of America's busiest cities.

Yet the entire fabric of white civilization in the tributary region is the fruit of hardly more than a century of time and toil. Chicago, the greatest city of interior America, celebrated her Century of Progress only a decade ago. The government agents who negotiated the Indian treaty of 1821 found not a single house between Peoria and Chicago. In 1823 a government exploring expedition was delayed for days at Chicago awaiting a guide who could conduct it across the wilderness to Prairie du Chien, Wisconsin. The first steamboats that ever visited Chicago came in 1832, bearing the soldiers who were to conclude the Black Hawk War, and on arriving they found no port or harbor, for neither then existed.

The westward-marching settler was now close at hand, however, and his rapid advance over the Upper Mississippi Valley is significantly registered in the organization of Wisconsin Territory in 1836, Iowa Territory in 1838, and Minnesota Territory in 1849, to be followed in each case by admission to statehood in a dozen years or less.

Although the settler came to subdue a wilderness, it was not a vacant land. For unrecorded ages the Red Man had occupied it, developing a Stone-age culture which made but slight use of the natural resources of the country and which knew nothing of material progress or change. The culture of the white man was utterly antipathetic to this, and when the two races came together the swift conquest and displacement of the red man by the white was inevitable. With variations of local detail the process was everywhere repeated as the settler moved westward across the Continent. Yet the Indian was a human being who genuinely loved his native land, and his conquest, however inevitable, involved much of grief and tragedy. At Rock Island the conflict was more than ordinarily dramatic. "I loved my towns, my cornfields, and the home of my people" said the fallen Black Hawk. "I fought for it . . . I have looked upon the Mississippi since I was a child. I love the great river. I have dwelt upon its banks since I was an infant."

The old-age narratives which are reprinted in the pages that follow the present introduction record the experiences and reflect the ideals and opinions of two early white settlers at the mouth of Rock River. John W. Spencer, whose *Reminiscences of Pioneer Life* is presented first, was a native of Vermont who in early manhood migrated to Illinois in 1820. As an early white settler he shared in all of the developments which culminated in the Black Hawk War of 1832, and his narrative is in large degree an old-age recital of that struggle. It seems evident that when he came to write it he endeavored to fortify his memory by reference to certain narratives which were already in print, and his own story is a mixture of personal knowledge and recollections with information derived from the sources of information already mentioned. Although the author achieved success in life, and bore the title of Judge, his story necessarily exhibits some of the defects which are inherent in old-age narratives of the type to which it belongs. It sheds interesting light upon the period it covers, telling us as much, perhaps, about the pioneer Illinois settler as it does about the red man whom he displaced.

The story told by John M. D. Burrows, unlike that of Spencer, relates, in intimate detail, the author's life and experiences throughout a period of fifty years. One of the earliest settlers of Davenport, and for most of this period one of that city's foremost businessmen, his narrative is an indispensable record of its first half-century of life. It also presents with unusual clarity the methods of conducting business and the vicissitudes encountered therein a century ago. Mr. Burrows was a man of remarkable energy, to whose vision and enterprise his community and time owes much, and it will be a sorry day for America when men of his type are prevented from exercising their talent for leadership by measures enacted by stupid men of lesser industry and daring.

Historical Introduction

For a picture of nineteenth-century pioneer America at its best, the author's story can scarcely be excelled.

Spencer's *Reminiscences of Pioneer Life in the Mississippi Valley*, "published for complimentary distribution, by his Children," was printed at Davenport in 1872. Burrows' *Fifty Years in Iowa* was printed at the same place in 1888. Like General Grant, a more famous contemporary, the author had fallen upon evil days, and he wrote his story in the hope that from its sale he might derive the means of support in his closing years. The two books are modest little volumes, whose circulation was necessarily limited, and neither of them has ever attracted any wide-spread attention. So far as we are aware, neither has ever before been reprinted. The present edition is a faithful reproduction of the originals save for the fact that the Editor has eliminated an occasional crudity of vocabulary or other obvious error; and has omitted from Mr. Burrows' narrative a two-page chapter telling the history of Oakdale Cemetery and a twenty-four page appendix devoted to the expulsion of the Mormons from Illinois and the murder of Colonel Davenport. The footnotes have been supplied by the present Editor.

M. M. QUAIFE

August 1, 1942

Reminiscences
of
Pioneer Life

REMINISCENCES

OF

PIONEER LIFE

IN THE

MISSISSIPPI VALLEY.

BY J. W. SPENCER.

Published for complimentary distribution, by his Children.

DAVENPORT:
GRIGGS, WATSON, & DAY, PRINTERS.
1872.

Preface

THE record of the Old Settlers can never be written. Nearly all of them are gone, and lie with the faded leaves which have fallen over their graves.

The history of the settlement of this part of the Mississippi Valley can never be recovered, as it was treasured only in the memories of those who came here before the Indians had been driven from their hunting grounds, to find new homes beyond the great river. The real character of the early settlers, and of the Indians, who have faded away before a stronger race, is well nigh lost: those who knew both classes being only represented here and there by a survivor, who has lived long beyond that hardy generation who here commenced the conquest of the wilderness.

To save a few pages of this early history—pages rendered even more valuable by the destruction of the rest—is the object of this publication.

To many, perhaps, who may read these lines, they may seem dry and uninteresting; for it is well nigh impossible that all should appreciate their importance, or understand the few tangled threads which have furnished the basis of the social culture into which they have since been woven.

Our time, in which bands of steel bind states together, and unseen cables send the thrill of thought from continent to continent —our time, when gold and plenty have introduced the arts and social life of sunnier lands, is far different from the stern life of the long ago, when the only bands were those of friendship, and the only electric thrill that of sympathy in common danger, which made all akin. The foundation of a palace may lack polish, but it must have strength. The stern struggles and painful privations of the early settlers developed that character which has given permanence and progress to the Great North-West. Here were laid the foundations of the Empire of the great rivers, which form now the central arteries of our continent.

To many, reared in this day of restless, hurrying life, these sketches will seem like a chapter from some long forgotten romance; like a picture of sunshine from some Arcadian valley.

Having heard, from childhood, the stories of the early day, and these, written out by the author, after his seventieth birthday, to be presented at the Old Settlers' meeting, and afterwards published in the UNION, the children of the author have desired them to be published, not for the general public, but for a permanent treasure for themselves, and for the pleasure of that limited audience who, by sufferings and privations on the frontier, have become capable of enjoying an Old Settler's story. It will be seen by the picture facing the title page, that, through the aid of a photographer, without the knowledge of the author, they are able to present to the friends who knew him in younger days, his picture as he looks now, showing the changes which a half century of pioneer life have wrought upon him.

Reminiscences of
Pioneer Life

———

I WAS born in Vergennes, Addison County,
Vermont, on the twenty-fifth of July,
1801, and after spending the early years
of my life there, started, on the fourth of
September, 1820, for Illinois, driving a two-
horse team for a gentleman by the name of
Brush.[1] Having an uncle in St. Louis County,
Missouri, I went there, crossing the Mississippi River on the twenty-fifth of October, at
St. Louis. This place had about five thousand inhabitants at that time. My uncle,
and many more of the early settlers, were
about leaving where they had settled, on account of Missouri becoming a slave state.
He and several of his neighbors had, early
in the fall of this year, visited the Illinois
River country, and made some selections for

[1] Mrs. Christiana H. Tillson, who made the similar
journey from Massachusetts to Illinois in 1822, devotes
many pages to the recital of her experiences encountered
en route. For her narrative, see *A Woman's Story of
Pioneer Illinois*, the Lakeside Classics volume for 1929,
pp. 31–73.

farms, about thirty miles from the mouth of the river, at a settlement now called Bluff-dale. In order to hold the lands they had selected, they were obliged to make some improvement on them, which, having done, they returned to Missouri.

About the first of December, in company with my cousin, who was five or six years my senior, with his wife and two children, we started for the Illinois River, where my uncle and his party had made their claims the fall before. On arriving there, we found on one of the claims a log cabin, about fourteen feet square, about half built; it lacked a roof, a floor, and a door, which we soon added. Our horses we fed, and for lack of a stable, turned loose at night. In hunting for them one morning, I found them about two miles from home, and as we turned on our way homeward I discovered a large bear on the bluff, headed for the river. When he got on the prairie bottom, I rode after him; the country being very smooth, I found I could drive him, so concluded to try and drive him home. Our cabin, at that time, was without a door, and for a substitute, they had hung up a blanket. The day being very windy, they had set a chest upon the blanket to keep it in place. This chest was a very considerable part of the furniture of the cabin, being used as a work table, a dining table, and a place for putting away our most valuable things. My cousin's wife was busy getting our breakfast, and had rolled out a short-cake upon the chest: he was at work outside the cabin, making a rude bedstead. On approaching the house I hallooed as loud as I could. The cabin stood in the timber, and my cousin did not discover the bear until he was within fifty yards of him. He ran in for his gun as soon as possible, and, by stepping on the chest at the door, and putting his gun over the blanket, he gave the bear a mortal wound the first fire. He then reloaded his gun, and going nearer him, fired a second shot, killing him. But this is not all; when his wife looked after her short-cake, she found that he had put his foot in it!

My neighbors in Greene County, some of whom accompanied Major Campbell, when he started from St. Louis, in the War of 1812, for the relief of the garrison of Prairie du Chien, gave me the particulars of this trip, which I do not think are familiar to our old settlers generally. We all know that there is an island near here named Campbell's Island, but few know why it bears this name. In 1812, Major Campbell, with three keelboats, well manned, and loaded with provisions for the relief of the garrison of Prairie du Chien, left St. Louis, and came along without being disturbed by Indians, until, at last, they reached Rock Island. They described the country here as being beautiful, finer than anything they had seen—and they landed on a prairie, at the foot of Rock Island, on the Illinois shore. The Indians came to the boats, and seemed friendly, trading some with them. The next morning, while sailing on the right side of Campbell's Island, the Major concluded to land for breakfast, against the wishes of his command. He landed his boat, and tied to the shore, the other two boats anchoring out in the stream.

As soon as the Major's boat was made fast, the Indians, who were concealed, commenced firing on them. These boats were so constructed that while the men were inside they were comparatively safe, but to cut their cable, so as to leave the shore, somebody must expose themselves. They sent out one after another to accomplish this purpose, until two or three had been shot down. Finding it so hazardous to extricate themselves in this way, they changed their plan, and by swinging the stern of the shore boat out, and that of the nearest boat at anchor in, they managed to get from the boat which was made fast to the shore into the other boats, some being killed, others wounded.

Among the wounded was Major Campbell, severely, in the shoulder. They now abandoned the boat at the shore, and the Indians, after plundering it, burned it. I have heard some of our first settlers say that in low water the wreck of this boat could be seen. Major Campbell was now forced to give up the trip, and returned to St. Louis with the remaining boats. By the failure of this expedition the garrison at Prairie du Chien was forced, for lack of provisions, to capitulate to the English, and the island near where these brave men were killed, and others wounded, was called Campbell's Island.[2] The Indians call a steamboat a fire-

[2] The author's narrative of Campbell's expedition is inaccurate in several respects. In July, 1814, a British-Indian army from Mackinac attacked and captured Fort Shelby at Prairie du Chien, Wis. Shortly before, and in ignorance of this affair, Lieut. John Campbell had set out from St. Louis in charge of a force of 120 soldiers in three keelboats to reinforce the Fort Shelby garrison. At Rock Island, on July 19, 1814, the rearmost boat grounded, and while thus handicapped was attacked by the near-by Sauk and Fox Indians. The two keelboats in advance returned to the relief of the stranded vessel, but one of them was set on fire and abandoned, while the other continued down river to St. Louis, leaving the occupants of the stranded boat to their fate. In this extremity the gunboat *General Clark*, retreating from its defeat at Prairie du Chien two days earlier, opportunely appeared on the scene and rescuing the beleaguered boatmen, took them back to

boat. At a dance of the Indians, on Rock Island, I heard Black Hawk, in making a little speech, allude to this boat; he said when this boat was burned it made a real "fire-boat." While living in this part of the state, Alton was our post office, being forty miles from our settlement.

About the year 1826, there was great excitement in regard to the lead mines of the upper Mississippi. In 1827 I thought I would try my luck one season at the mines. I passed Rock Island, on my way up the river, about the last of March, returning late in the summer.

This practice of going up the river in the spring and coming down in the fall, was so generally observed by the first settlers of Illinois, that they were called "Suckers."[3]

St. Louis. In the fight at Campbell's Island 16 Americans were killed and 21 were wounded. Upon the receipt at St. Louis of the news of Campbell's disaster, Major Zachary Taylor with 330 men in eight gunboats set out for Rock Island to punish the savages, only to meet with another defeat on September 5.

[3] Because of the habit of the sucker of ascending rivers in the spring and descending them in the autumn. Since many of the miners "holed-in" for the winter at the lead mines, in sod houses or other huts, they were called "Badgers," which became the popular nickname of the people of Wisconsin. The present Editor does not undertake to certify the truth of these explanations, however. They are a part of the local folklore which defies scholarly verification.

In the fall of 1828 I removed to Morgan County, about twelve miles from Jacksonville, on the Beardstown Road. Mr. Rinnah Wells, in passing from the mines to the southern part of the state, stopped with me over night. In the course of the evening he told me that the Indians had left their old village at Rock Island. Having seen the country along the Rock Island Rapids in passing to and from the mines, and being much pleased with it, in less than a week, accompanied by Loudon Case, Sr., I was on my way to ascertain if the Indians had left. When about ten miles from Rock River, we met a Mr. Prince, who had brought a load of corn from his farm near Peoria, to feed Judge Pence's team, who was just then moving to the old Indian village at Rock River. Princeville on the Peoria Railroad, bears his name. We reached Rock River on the 9th of December. The river seemed alive with ducks. I do not think I have ever seen as many at one time since. Getting on the track of Judge Pence's wagons we crossed to the Big Island. Here we found Judge Pence looking for a place to ford, which we found about sundown, between the upper bridge and mill-dam, on the main stream. Here we found several wigwams, and took shelter in a large one for the night. Early in the morning Judge Pence started out, and returned about breakfast time, saying he would not unload his wagon here, as he had found a better wigwam, which proved to be Black Hawk's. These wigwams are very much the shape of a New England barn, sixteen or eighteen feet wide, and from twenty to fifty or sixty feet long. The largest were calculated for from two to four families. They were built by setting posts in the ground, and siding with bark from elm trees. This bark, cut about seven feet long, varied in width from two to four feet, according to the size of the tree taken from. They had rafters, and on these were laid small poles, upon the poles was placed the bark, making a roof that turned rain very well. These wigwams made a very comfortable summer house. Their wigwams for fall and winter use were very different, being of flags woven into matting, which could be rolled up, and enough to cover a wigwam carried on one horse. They made a frame of small poles, one end sharpened and stuck in the ground, the other bent over so as to form a circle of ten or twelve feet. Then they placed the matting around and over the poles, leaving a small opening in the top for the smoke. A little fire in the center would keep the wigwam warm. The Indians say "the white man makes a great fire, and stands a great way off, the Indian makes a little fire, and gets very near it." On our arrival here we found no Indians, it being the season of the year when they were absent on their winter's hunt. The settlers, as well as the officers of the garrison, thought they would not return. We found here two white families, near where the Farnam house stood, one of them Captain Clark, father of Captain Louis Clark, of Buffalo, Scott County, Iowa, the other a discharged soldier by the name of Haney; Judge Pence at Rock River; and at the Rapids, where Rapids City now stands, were John and Thomas Kinney, George Harlan, Conrad Lee, and Archibald Allen. This constituted all the white settlement on the main land. North about seventy miles, on the Plum River, was a family by the name of Davidson; two miles below New Boston, was a family by the name of Dennison, and on the Lower Rapids was old Jim White. At this time they only had an occasional mail here, which was got by sending two soldiers on foot to Galena. Soon after I came, having business at Galena, and the officers of the garrison being anxious to hear who had been elected President, in November, it being now the 20th of December, it was arranged that I should carry the mail to Galena, and bring one in return, for which I was to receive five dollars.

17

This trip had to be made on foot, as I had sent my team home. So they fitted me out with a knapsack, and taking a pair of skates, I started on my trip, stopping the first night at the head of the Rapids. From this point to Mr. Davidson's, the first house, was about fifty miles, and the days being the shortest of the year, it required some energy to reach this house, which would make a good stopping place for the night. In the course of the day I met a large party of Winnebago, who were moving and were traveling across my track. I was not then much acquainted with the Indians, and hardly knew what would be the best course to pursue, but concluded it was best to pass right along among them, as though I was not at all disturbed. They gathered around me, and all I could understand was that they wanted bread. I was skating along, at that time, on a large pond, and the Indian boys followed after me, very much pleased with this, to them, novel way of going. Before reaching Plum River, it was dark, and as the house I wanted to reach was a mile on the other side, the river must be crossed. I tried the ice, and found that it would not bear me, and concluded to camp for the night. It being a prairie, and no wood near, I remembered to have seen some driftwood about a half mile back, and returned there to camp for the night.

Now came the feat of making a fire on a dark night. I put my hat on the ground, with the top up, putting some cotton on the hat and sprinkling some powder on the cotton; then took my knife and flint, and tried to make fire. Not succeeding very well, I poured a little more powder on the cotton; it being very dark and cold, and feeling a little uncertain about my success in making fire, and knowing the great importance of having a fire in camping in winter, I repeated the operation two or three times. At last, getting very anxious, I got my face down very near the hat, and with my knife and flint succeeded in igniting the powder. I thought at first my eyes were nearly put out, but it being very necessary to save my fire, I succeeded in doing so.

In the morning I followed up the river until I found a place so narrow that I made a crossing. This took me so far out of my way that I did not stop at Mr. Davidson's at all going up. I reached Galena safely, exchanged the mails, transacted my other business, and about noon, on Christmas day started on my return. Traveling about twenty miles I came to a wood chopper's camp, and stayed all night. The next morning I breakfasted at Mr. Davidson's, at Plum River.[4] This was

[4] The Davidson and Pierce families (interrelated) settled at the site of present-day Savanna about Novem-

a very excellent family, but I found only
Mrs. Davidson at home. After breakfast I
asked her how much I owed her—she replied,
"a quarter." I gave her a half dollar, but
she could not change it and refused to keep
the whole of it. Meeting with her husband
in 1832, I told him I was indebted to him.
He said he did not know it. When I related
the circumstances he remarked, "You are a
pretty honest fellow."

Leaving Plum River, I camped two miles
or more this side of the Meridosia. All night
I could hear the wolves walking about me,
and could hear the Indian dogs barking, as
there were Indians on an island in the river.

The next day I reached the fort at Rock
Island, delivering the mail, and bringing the
news of the election of General Jackson.

In coming into the village when I first
came here I noticed a number of poles standing, from twenty to thirty feet high. Some
of these poles had branches or limbs left on
them, on which were hung small gourds. I
have seen, when the Indians returned from
their winter hunt, a dead dog tied up to one

ber 1, 1828, becoming thereby the first settlers of Carroll County. At the time of Spencer's visit they had
been in the place only a few weeks. For the story of
their settlement see Chas. L. Hostetter, *Hist. of Carroll
County* (Chicago, 1913), 634, 654–55.

of these poles, by winding a rope several times around the pole and dog, the head being up. I always supposed this to be a religious ceremony. Every time they succeeded in battle and none of their number was killed, a new pole was erected, and upon the pole were hung some of the trophies of the victory, and around it the successful warriors and women danced. But if in the battle they lost any of their number, even if they had killed a great number of the enemy, there was no dancing or any demonstrations of joy.

The first season I lived here, about forty of our Indians swam the Missouri River in the night, broke into an encampment of one hundred of the Sioux lodges, and killed fifteen of them with their knives, losing two of their own number. On account of their loss, there was no dancing or any rejoicing, but when they came home they blackened their faces and mourned the loss of their two braves. The same season, three of our Indians, on a scout on the Missouri, discovered an Omaha Indian on the prairie. They told me they got into a low, bushy tree, and bleated like a deer, bringing the man near, when they shot and killed him. This Indian had a gun and bridle with him; these, with his scalp, they brought home with them.

Now was explained to me the use of these

poles. A new one was erected, and the gun and bridle hung on the pole. Then they began to dance around it—that is, the three men who killed the Indian, and several of the squaws. At these dances none of the men except those who actually participated in the battle danced; but the young men, gaily painted, stood looking on. One of the squaws carried the scalp on a stick, about four feet above her head. For music, they had a drum made by taking out the head of a powder keg and stretching a raw hide over it. Some one of the old men, with one drum-stick, such as is used on a bass drum, beat with a slow, measured stroke, while several old men, sitting on the ground, accompanied the drum by singing. This music, in a still night, could be heard three or four miles. The dancers kept up the entertainment for two or three days, until entire exhaustion ensued. At intervals during the rejoicing, the music and dancing would stop, and a man would step forward—usually an old man—with a tomahawk or some other instrument of war in his hand, and make a little speech, telling of some war exploit, the Indians all responding with a general shout. Then the music and dancing were again resumed. I witnessed this performance several times while the Indians were here.

After coming, in the fall of 1828, and making my selection for a farm, I moved from Morgan County, arriving here on the first day of March, 1829. As there was no house to be had, the next best chance was a wigwam. We found one on the bluff, near where Henry Case now lives, which we thought we could use until we could build a cabin. This same spring there came Louden Case, Sr., and his three sons—Jonah, Louden, and Charles—and settled at the old Case place. Rinnah Wells and his four sons, and Joshua Vandruff and sons settled at Rock River. In January, before, Joel Wells settled near Hampton, and in the spring Joel Wells, Sr., and Levi and Huntington Wells settled at Moline; Joseph Danforth, a son-in-law of Rinnah Wells, a mile above Moline; and Michael C. Bartlett, a son-in-law of Joel Wells, Sr., about where the quilt factory now stands. About the last of May came Mr. Goble and his son Benjamin, settling above Joseph Danforth. Wm. T. Brashar settled on the farm bearing his name.

We were here but a few days when two Indians came—the first we had seen. One of them commenced talking in a loud voice in the Indian language, of which we could not understand a word. By pointing to the wigwam, saying "Saukie wigeop," then pointing to the ground, saying "Saukie aukie," and repeating this many times, we understood he claimed the land and the wigwam belonged to the Indians. This man proved to be Black Hawk. We had never heard there was such a chief.[5] He had heard, way out at his winter hunting grounds, that the white man had taken possession of their lands and their wigwams; and he, with the Indian who accompanied him, had walked in all the way, to find the report too true. He first went to his own wigwam, which he found occupied by Judge Pence. This wigwam stood about one hundred yards in front of Rinnah Wells's house, at Rock River. Black Hawk seemed to be very much plagued to find his wigwam occupied, and showed Judge Pence where the fire had burned the posts of the wigwam, and gave them to understand that if they were to have such great fires they ought to protect the posts. Coming from his own wigwam over to where we lived, it is not to be wondered at that the old man was somewhat excited. About six weeks after Black

[5] Either this interview or another held under practically identical circumstances is described by Black Hawk himself in his *Life* (Lakeside Classics ed., Chicago, 1916), 104–106. The author's statement that the settlers had never heard of Black Hawk is difficult to credit.

Hawk's visit here, he, with the rest of the Indians, returned, and by this time Judge Pence was living in his own cabin, in their village. They were very much displeased to find white settlers so near them, and about two hundred of their young men mounted their horses and rode around Judge Pence's house several times. Mrs. Pence and the children, being alone, were very much alarmed, having never seen so many Indians before. She succeeded in sending one of the children to the fort on the island for help. The Indian agent being absent, Captain Nelson, in command, sent down the interpreter, Antoine Le Claire, who told the Indians they must behave, or they would be visited by the soldiers. They soon became quiet, and we got along pretty well during the season, except a little trouble between the Indians and Rinnah Wells.

The Indians planted their corn in the same hill for many years. They scraped off the outside with a hoe, then dug up the hill thoroughly, and placed the corn in the hill with the hand. They cultivated it altogether with a hoe, going over it three or four times, making the hills very large. After forty years, they are now plainly to be seen in the old fields. They raised a good many beans of a fine quality; also squashes, and a

few melons. This was their entire crop. This
work was done mostly by the squaws. I have
seen some old men, and some boys of twelve
or fifteen years, working in the field, but
only one young or middle-aged man, and he
was making a fence. Their cultivated grounds
were fenced by sticking stakes in the ground
and tying poles to them, making a very weak
fence, that would not turn cattle or hogs.

One day a party of three or four of us
called upon Keokuk,[6] feeling that he was
friendly to us, and offered to plow his field.
He accepted our proposition, and came out
frequently and treated us to sweetened water,
which was made by putting maple sugar in
the water, and was considered by the Indians
a very nice drink.

In the spring of 1829, when the corn was
about knee-high, Keokuk called on all the
white settlers and proposed that they should
put up their cattle at night, on account of
the Indians' poor fences, and said the Indians would watch them in the daytime, and
the cattle should not be hurt. All the settlers
agreed to this proposition except Mr. Rinnah

[6] Keokuk, Black Hawk's rival, was the leader of the
faction among the Sauk and Foxes which acquiesced in
the demand of the white authorities that they abandon
their homes at Rock Island and remove west of the
Mississippi. See *Life* of Black Hawk, 103-107.

Wells, who thought it too much trouble. When the corn got in good order for roasting ears, Mr. Wells's cattle came out one night to near Mr. Corker's old place, and ate up the corn of several Indian families. Mr. Wells had corn on the opposite side of the road—the road running about as it does now. The next night, when the cattle returned for another meal, the Indians turned them into Mr. Wells's own field. After that, Mr. Wells took care of his cattle.

I became very well acquainted with Black Hawk, living, one summer, less than a quarter of a mile from him. He was a man of medium size, and about sixty years of age—a very quiet, peaceable neighbor. Black Hawk was a strong temperance man. In all my acquaintance with him, I never knew him to have but one spree. The first summer I lived here, Black Hawk, accompanied by a few of his braves, made a visit to a man selling whisky to Indians. He rolled the barrels out doors, and with his tomahawk knocked in the heads and let the whisky out.[7] For this he was called to account by the Indian agent, who told him such conduct would not be allowed, and that it would bring him in conflict with the government. After leaving the

[7] For Black Hawk's own account of this affair see his *Life*, 108.

council house, I heard him tell the interpreter, Mr. Le Claire, that he believed he would not get himself into any more trouble of this kind, as by the effort to keep his young men from drinking he had made himself a great deal of trouble. As for himself, he said he would not drink and would wear wampum, but the young men might drink and wear swansdown—meaning, he would save his property, and they might drink and spend theirs. After he was deposed by the government, he never tried to influence the Indians, or take any part in their business.

Before the war I never knew him to wear any part of a white man's garb, but after it he wore a coat, hat, and pants.

It was the practice of our Indians to leave here for their fall and winter hunting grounds about the middle of September, and return about the middle of April. They all left on the same day, if not the same hour. In order to move in this way, it was arranged that a man with a strong voice, several days before leaving, went through the village telling them on such a day they would leave for their winter hunting grounds.

Our Indians consisted of the Sauk and Foxes, these two tribes owning their lands jointly. I noticed that when they traveled they camped separately. The Foxes, while living here, lived from Jonah Case's old place up as far as Wm. Brooks's. The Foxes had mostly left previous to my coming here, except a few who had intermarried with the Sauk, and had made villages at Princeton, Bellevue, and Dubuque.

Our Indians, in starting for their hunting grounds, went down the river with the help of their horses, of which they had five or six hundred, and their canoes, which numbered about two hundred.

Before starting it was understood by the two tribes where each should go, so as to avoid confusion. In hunting the Sauk occupied southern and middle Iowa, the Foxes northern Iowa. Our Indians ascended the Iowa, Skunk, Des Moines, and all smaller streams that would admit of a canoe. After the fall hunt they had a rendezvous appointed, where they assembled for winter quarters. This selection was made in a large timbered bottom, on account of their horses, and security from the Sioux.

They sometimes made temporary forts as a protection against the enemy. After making their maple sugar in the spring, they were now ready to start for the old village. As soon as possible, they would gather on the Mississippi, those that went to the more northern streams would wait for those who

went farther south. They would all gather
together about the Iowa River and move up
the river, waiting for bad weather, making
at best not more than eight or ten miles a
day. They had a leader, who permitted no
straggling, having it understood in the morning where they would camp at night. So in
the greatest order, keeping the canoes and
horses as near together as possible, they
would arrive here the same hour.

They brought home little besides the sugar
just made and dried meat, their skins and
furs having been disposed of to the Indian
traders where they had been. Now they
commenced looking for their corn, beans,
and dried squashes they had cached in the
fall. This was done by good hiding. The
most common way was to select a dry piece
of ground where there was a blue grass sod.
They then cut out a circular sod about
eighteen inches in circumference, or as large
as would admit a person's body. This sod
was laid aside, and then a large hole dug,
enlarging as they went down, to the depth of
five or six feet, so as to make it of sufficient
size to hold the corn, beans, squashes, and
sometimes crab apples of one family. These
were put in sacks of their own making. They
then put in bark on the bottom and sides,
and inside of this they put these sacks of pro-

visions, for the next spring's use. Then they were covered with bark and filled with dirt, and the sod was carefully replaced, so as to make it look perfectly natural. They then cleaned up all the surplus dirt and hid it away, so there was nothing to indicate that anything had been buried there, or the earth disturbed at all. It depended on the hiding whether there would be any corn in the spring, for as soon as they were gone the Winnebago and other Indians came here hunting for their treasure. These Indians, by the aid of their muskrat spears, feeling in the ground, often succeeded in finding, and would take the supplies of several families.

One family with whom I was acquainted, buried their supplies in the center of their wigwam, where they had their fire. After burying their treasure they had made a large fire to make it look all right. But the Winnebago hunted around and stuck their spears in the ground, and finally discovered the place, and took it all. The old squaw to whom it belonged wept bitterly.

When a family had been robbed in this way of all they had, it was the custom to send some of the young men around the village, from one wigwam to another, and collect a small quantity of each one for the sufferers. This robbery made no disturbance

31

between the different tribes. A large part of the corn had been boiled and cut from the cob, and dried when green, making very nice eating, which they enjoyed very much, eating nearly all the time for several days, being deprived of this kind of food for some time before they came home. The Indians made one buffalo hunt each year, leaving home the first of July.

This required a good deal of preparation, as they went a long distance, and into the Sioux country, their deadly enemy. Each man was armed with a gun, bow, and a large bundle of arrows. They expected fighting, and generally brought home scalps, dried meat, and tallow, but no robes, on account of the hot weather. There happened this year a circumstance of some note. Our Indians, in an attack on the Sioux camp on Turkey River, near where Dubuque now stands, killed several Sioux, and among the rest a Winnebago squaw and a Menominee boy. They hastened to the Winnebago, and settled their mistake by giving them some horses. This seems to be the currency of the Indians. They always seemed to wish to avoid a rupture with the Winnebago, who were 8,000 strong.[8] The Menominee spoke

[8] Although the Winnebago were a powerful tribe, this estimate of their number is probably unduly high. De-

the same language, and were particular
friends, and being a long distance away,
they put off settling with them until the next
spring, when nine of the principal men of the
Foxes, of the Dubuque village, started in a
canoe for Prairie du Chien, to make the settlement for killing the boy. When a little
below the Wisconsin River they were attacked by the Menominee and all killed.[9]
This stirred up the spirit of revenge, and in
August our Indians surprised the Menominee
within three hundred yards of Fort Crawford, at Prairie du Chien, and killed forty-six
of them, men, women, and children.[10] Our
government called our Indians to an account
for this, as they had the right to do by a
former treaty, which was to the effect that
all differences between these tribes should
be submitted to it for settlement. On being
called up, Keokuk took a stick and balanced

scendants of the tribe still reside, in considerable numbers, in Wisconsin and Nebraska. For an intimate and
sympathetic picture of the Winnebago see Mrs. John H.
Kinzie's *Wau-Bun*, the Lakeside Classics volume for
1932.

[9] This slaughter took place in May, 1830. See *Wis.
Hist. Colls.*, V, 256–57; IX, 324–26.

[10] This massacre occurred in the summer of 1831.
John H. Fonda, who helped bury the Menominee,
places the number slain at 28. See *Wis. Hist. Colls.*, V,
257–58.

it on his hand, and said: "Put these nine principal men of the Foxes on one end, and the forty-six women and children of the Menominee on the other end, and I think it will be a fair settlement." And that was the settlement.

The possessions of the Sauk and Foxes in Illinois commenced at the mouth of the Illinois River, keeping along that stream as far as Peoria, then moving north so as to strike the Wisconsin River seventy or eighty miles from its mouth, down the Wisconsin to the Mississippi, and down the Mississippi to the place of beginning. On the west side of the Mississippi, they owned the whole of what is now the state of Iowa. Colonel Davenport[11] informed me, as nearly as he could ascertain, our Indians originally occupied the country about Montreal, Canada; from there they removed to Green Bay, possibly about two hundred years ago; and, as nearly as he could ascertain, they had been living here about sixty years when I came here. From

---

[11] George Davenport, one of the founders of the city which bears his name, came to Rock Island in 1816, when Fort Armstrong was established. He engaged in the Indian trade, became postmaster in 1825, and in 1835 joined with associates in laying out the town of Davenport. He was murdered in his home overlooking the Mississippi at Rock Island, July 4, 1845. See *Dict. Am. Biog.*

the growth of timber, from their corn-fields,
and from every indication by which a frontier man judges of the age of a settlement, I
have no doubt but his information was correct. Now they had at last reached the great
Father of Waters, the most beautiful country their eyes had ever seen. The rivers
abounded in fish, and the country was alive
with game; and they were not willing to be
driven so unjustly from these their fruitful
hunting grounds.[12]

There is an old legend, said to be believed
by the Indians, in regard to the Island, and
this was another reason why they so much
disliked to give up that beautiful spot, to be
made a military post. They had been taught
to believe that a Good Spirit had the care of
it, who lived in a cave in the rocks immediately under the place where the fort was

[12] This sketch of the history of the Sauk and Foxes,
although inadequate, is reasonably correct. Prior to the
coming of the French to the Georgian Bay area (c.
1625-40) they were living in the Michigan Lower Pen-
insula, where they have given permanent names to
Saginaw Bay and River. Pressed by the Iroquois, they
migrated to the Green Bay region, where the earliest
French visitors encountered them, about 1665-70.
Long continued warfare with the French resulted in their
further migration, about the middle of the eighteenth
century, to the Upper Mississippi area. They had been
at Rock Island probably 80-100 years at the time of the
author's advent in 1828.

built. He is said to have been often seen by the Indians, and was white, with wings like a swan, but ten times larger. The Island was much frequented by them in summer, but they were always careful to make no noise in the part of the island which he inhabited. They believed the noise and confusion incident to building and maintaining the fort drove him away.

The Indians were governed by two sets of chiefs—peace or civil chiefs, and war chiefs. The duties of the peace chiefs were to settle all troubles between their tribes and other tribes, and also between them and the whites; while the war chiefs never interfered, in any particular, in the business of the village. The two prominent war chiefs, when I came here, were Black Hawk and Keokuk. In times of trouble, the prominent war and peace chiefs consulted together, and there was the most perfect understanding as to the management of affairs.

When we consider that these tribes were only about two thousand strong, and held their lands by their prowess as warriors, it gives us some idea of their fighting qualities.

In 1804 one of our Indians killed a man in St. Louis, and was put in jail. A deputation of five principal men from here went to St. Louis, expecting to get him released by giv-

ing horses for him, as was the custom among
the Indians. While these men were in St.
Louis they sold all of their lands on the east
side of the Mississippi River, the government agreeing to pay them $2,000 a year
forever. Old General Clark, the partner of
Lewis in crossing the Rocky Mountains, was
the general superintendent of the western
Indians at that time, acting for the government.[13]

Colonel Davenport told me that he did not
believe Black Hawk ever took a pipe-full of
tobacco bought with that money. He and a
large part of the Indians were bitterly opposed to this sale. Out of this sale grew the
Black Hawk War; Black Hawk and his party
contending that the lands were not sold, as
the men who made the sale were not au-
thorized to sell, but went to St. Louis on
other business. There was a clause in the
sale that the Indians might occupy the land
while it belonged to the government. The
land had been surveyed several years before
I came here, and before the Indians left in

---

[13] This is an error. William Clark, subsequently Governor of Missouri Territory and Indian Superintendent,
was absent on the transcontinental exploring expedition
(1803–1806) when the treaty was negotiated by Governor William Henry Harrison of Indiana Territory in
November, 1804.

the fall there was a notice given that the lands would be offered for sale in October, and the Indian agent told them they must not come back. It was hoped by the settlers that the Indians would not return, but in this they were disappointed, for they came as usual, though not as many as before. Keokuk and his followers did not return. He was opposed to their coming back, and commenced a village on the Iowa River, about twenty miles from its mouth. Keokuk was the head or chief of what was called the American party. He was not the son of a chief, but attained his rank by his ability and talent, being a remarkable orator.

Black Hawk was a born chief, belonging to a royal family, and was the head of what was known as the British party.[14]

The year of 1830 passed off very well, considering the situation of the whites and Indians. During the summer our Indians re-

[14] Authorities differ in affirming, or denying, that Black Hawk was a chief. According to R. G. Thwaites ("Story of the Black Hawk War," in *Wis. Hist. Colls.*, XII, 219) "he was neither an hereditary nor an elected chief, but was by common consent the leader of his village." Frank E. Stevens (*The Black Hawk War*, 21) says his father was the tribal medicine man "and whatever standing Black Hawk may have secured was derived from his personal bravery and daring as a warrior, which have never been questioned."

ceived a visit from sixteen young men of the
Kickapoo. They were from twenty to
twenty-five years of age. This summer I
lived at the old village, having good opportunity to see all that transpired between the
Indians. The Kickapoo spoke the same language as our Indians, as well as several other
tribes. They entertained their guests right
royally, keeping them all at one large wigwam, making it very pleasant for them.

I wondered how so many could be entertained at one place, knowing that the Indians' supplies were quite limited. Mr.
Nathan Smith, who lived with the Indians,
explained it to me in this way. He said they
were the guests of the entire village, and that
two of the young men would go through the
village and collect provisions from the different wigwams, for their entertainment, this
being repeated as often as necessary, while
they remained. These young men stayed
about a month, having a splendid time.
About the last of their stay they took one
day to visit each wigwam in the village, at
which they danced and were treated to something to eat, and generally some sweetened
water to drink. When these young Indians
came they were on foot, but our Indians,
after entertaining them so handsomely, gave
each one a horse when they left for home.

In 1831 came a new era in our history. The Indians returned in large numbers, perhaps as many as in 1829, and with quite a different spirit towards the whites. Black Hawk gave the settlers to understand that after this season they must go south of Rock River, or above Pleasant Valley. He said this district between the rivers should be occupied exclusively by the Indians, giving several reasons why they could not afford to give up these pleasant hunting grounds. One reason was that on this side of the Mississippi they were comparatively safe from their enemies, and another, that the region abounded with game and fish, and was suited to their mode of living, and they would not give it up. Black Hawk said we could all stay this season, except Joshua Vandruff and Rinnah Wells, who lived in the midst of their village, and had a large stock of cattle, which troubled the Indians a great deal. Mr. Vandruff showed Black Hawk that it would be very hard for him to leave on so short a notice, as he was a poor man, and had twelve children. Black Hawk finally consented that he could stay another season, but Mr. Wells must go, and he would give him until the next day to make his choice whether he would go willingly or be put off. Mr. Wells consulted with his friends, and finally con-

sented to leave in thirty days. This move on
the part of the Indians made it necessary for
the settlers to look about and see what they
could do for their protection.

We had petitioned the Governor of the
state in the summer of 1829 without his taking any notice, but now we concluded to try
it again. We made a statement of our griev-
ances, and of the order of Black Hawk for
our removal, and forwarded it with all possible haste to the Governor.[15] This had the
desired effect. The Governor moved immediately, going first to Jefferson Barracks,
Missouri, where he found Old General
Gaines. He told the General that if he
would go to Rock Island and drive the Indians out of the state he would give him the
job; but if he would not or could not go, he
would do it himself. The General concluded
to undertake the business, and, taking the
Sixth Regiment, which was then lying at
Jefferson Barracks, he proceeded at once to
Rock Island. When here, he commenced firing morning and evening guns, which had
not been the practice; also, target shooting

---

[15] This petition, dated May 19, 1831, is printed in
Frank E. Stevens, *The Black Hawk War* (Chicago,
1903), 83. An earlier petition (April 30, 1831), printed
on p. 82, may be the one which the author alludes to as
having been submitted to the Governor in 1829.

with his cannon. He had all the white settlers come into the fort, bringing all their
horses and cattle on to the Island as expedi-
tiously as possible. When this was done, he
sent for Black Hawk for a talk with him
about the village, and a day was fixed for a
meeting.

Keokuk and some of his friends came up
from their village, on the Iowa River, and
came on to the Island. General Gaines, the
officers of the Sixth Regiment, the officers of
the garrison, with the citizens, and Keokuk
and his friends, met in the Council House.
Black Hawk, with seventy-five to one hundred warriors, nicely dressed and painted,
drew near. When within about one hundred
yards of the Council House they commenced
singing in a very loud voice, which seemed to
alarm Keokuk and party so much that they
left in great haste. Those who understood
the Indians best, thought, from the singing
and the manner of the Indians, that there
would be a general massacre. A man that
always accompanied Black Hawk, as they
entered the Council House, commenced singing in a very boisterous manner, and gesticu-
lating as though he was very angry, speaking
very rapidly. General Gaines spoke to him
very quietly of the sale of their lands. The
Indian said the land had never been sold.

General Gaines then called for the reading of the treaty, which seemed to enrage him still more. He said, "The white people speak from a paper; but," he added, striking his hand upon his breast, "the Indians always speak from the heart."

After the purchase of these lands from the Indians, in 1804, the Government had exchanged all the lands north of the old Indian boundary line (ranging from the most southern bend of Lake Michigan due west to the Mississippi, striking the river about where the boat-yard now is, in the lower end of town), with the Chippewa, Potawatomi, and Ottawa, for land lying about Chicago.

In 1829 the Government re-purchased these lands of the Indians, giving them $16,000 a year forever (that is the way the treaty reads), and allowing them to select a quarter section for each of their half-breeds. These selections amounted to a great deal of very valuable land. Antoine Le Claire and brother selected theirs on the Mississippi River, commencing at Moline and running up as far as Henry McNeil's old place.

The first point Black Hawk tried to make when he spoke was, that "the land had not been sold, as the men who went to St. Louis had no authority to sell, having been sent on other business." By this time we began to

think Black Hawk was pretty nearly right.
The second point he made was, "if it was
sold, they had got nothing for it." He said,
over and over again, "if a small part of the
land was worth $16,000 a year forever, all of
it must be worth more than $2,000." When
the General pressed an answer about his
leaving, he said all the time, "he would not
fight, and he would not leave, but if our people came to drive him off he would sit down
in his wigwam, and they might do what they
pleased with him; for himself he would do
nothing." General Gaines interpreted his
talk to mean that he would fight.

The General's force was very small—only
about five hundred men in all—consisting of
the Sixth Regiment, not full, and two companies that belonged at the garrison. The
men and boys of the settlement were all at
the fort, away from their homes, doing nothing. I went with another citizen and called
on the General, and proposed that the men
and boys of the settlement be formed into a
company, which was accordingly done. The
company numbered fifty-eight men, and was
called the Rock River Rangers. We were
mustered into service the 5th of June, 1831.

An election of officers was held, which resulted in the election of Benjamin J. Pike as
captain; John W. Spencer, first lieutenant;

Griffith Aubrey, second lieutenant; James Haskill, Leonard Bryant, and Edward Corbin, sergeants; Charles French, Charles Case, Benjamin Goble, and Henry Benson, corporals.

The members of the company were:—

Allen, Archibald	Noble, Amos C.
Brashar, Wm. T.	Syms, Thomas
Bane, John	Syms, Robert
Bartlett, Michael	Sams, Wm. F.
Been, Joseph	Smith, Martin W.
Case, Jonah H.	Stringfield, Sevier
Danforth, Joseph	Thompson, Joel
Davis, Thomas	Vandruff, Joshua
Dance, Russell	Vandruff, Henry
Frith, Isaiah	Vandruff, Samuel
Gardner, Thomas	Vannetta, Benjamin
Harlan, George W.	Vannetta, Gorham
Hultz, Uriah S.	Varner, Edward
Hubbard, Thomas	Wells, Levi
Hubbard, Goodridge	Wells, George
Henderson, Cyrus	Wells, Joel, Sr.
Johnson, Moses	Wells, Joel, Jr.,
Kinney, John W.	Wells, Huntington
Kinney, Samuel	Wells, John
Leek, Conrad	Wells, Samuel
Levit, Thomas	Wells, Rinnah
McNeil, Henry	Wells, Asaph
Miller, George	Wells, Eri
McGee, Gentry	Wells, Ira

General Gaines now called on the Governor for help, and he collected about 1,600 mounted men, with a rendezvous at Beardstown.

At a second meeting with Black Hawk, he brought up an old Indian by the name of Quashquama, or Jumping Fish, who was one of the five men who sold the land. He was a very old man, and seemed to be in his second childhood, and to have lost all memory of the sale. He was the only one of the five living, and his testimony was of no use.

At the fourth and last meeting came a middle-aged squaw, who introduced herself to the General, and said she was a grand-daughter of a prominent chief, and then began to speak of the sale of the lands. She said "the men could not sell the cornfields, for they belonged to the women—they had made them." She said, "it was very hard work to dig up the ground," and putting her hand on her back, she said, "it made their backs ache." Another reason she gave was, "that if the men had sold them they would have told them of it, which they had never done."

While they were waiting for the arrival of help and parleying with the Indians, General Gaines fitted up the steamboat *Winnebago* with a cannon on the bow of the boat, and a company of soldiers, and proceeded up Rock River to their village, passing within fifty yards of their wigwams. Strange to say, although a steamboat was seldom seen in those days, the Indians seemed not to take the least notice of the boat, not even looking at it, and even the women and children showed no signs of wonder or fear.

As soon as the Governor's troops were collected together, they marched for Rock Island, camping the last night within about ten miles of the Island. The Indians, being aware of their approach, crossed the Mississippi at night, taking with them all their effects, women, children, horses, and dogs.[16] The next day was fixed for the attack upon Black Hawk. It was arranged that General Gaines should take the boat, with one company of men from the garrison, and ascend Rock River, while Major Bliss, with the rest of the forces, should cross over and form on this side, and march for Rock River. Just about where the Rock Island Railroad freight house now stands, we were met by an Indian named Black Buffalo, a man I knew very well. He had a bridle in his hand, and was hunting his horse.

He had swapped horses with Jonas H. Case, the year before; the horse did not like

---

[16] This withdrawal west of the Mississippi took place in the night of June 25–26, 1831. For an excellent account of the entire war which followed, see T. C. Pease, *The Frontier State, 1818–1848* (Springfield, 1918), Chap. VIII.

to go with the Indians, and had given them the slip. Major Bliss wished me to ask him about the Indians, where they were, &c. He told me they had all crossed the Mississippi. The Major told me to tell him if he did not tell the truth he would kill him. The Indian still affirmed that what he said was true. He was sent to the fort a prisoner for that day.

Major Bliss formed our company of Rock River Rangers in an extended line of half a mile, in front of the regulars, with one cannon in the rear, for our march for Rock River. We marched near where the road is now traveled, until we reached General Rodman's land, then turned to the left until we reached the top of the bluff, taking the direction of Black Hawk's Watch Tower. On arriving there, we planted the cannon on the brow of the bluff, and then commenced throwing grape and canister into the bushes on Vandruff's Island. It was here we expected to find the Indians. General Gaines arrived with the boat and stopped about where the bridge crosses the main stream, near Sears' flouring mill, and commenced firing on the Island also. This island was very bushy, and commanded the only ford that the Governor and his forces could cross at. But it proved that Black Buffalo had told the truth. The Governor's troops, after crossing the river, burned the Indians' wigwams, and marched for Rock Island, and camped on the river, from the ferry landing to the freight house. This force amounted to 1,600 mounted men. They turned their 1,600 horses loose on the prairie, and the next thing was to procure fuel to cook their supper. I had a field of twenty acres of corn and potatoes, and the volunteers went for the fence. We tried to stop them from taking the rails, but could not; going to the Governor and General Gaines, they went out to the field and told the men they must not take the fence. While they were present the men stopped operations, but as soon as they turned to return the men, to the number of four or five hundred, took each a rail on his shoulder, and marched behind them into camp. By this operation I lost all my crop for one year, for which I never received a cent, the soldiers doing me ten times as much damage as the Indians had ever done. When we asked Black Hawk why he did not do as he said he would, "sit down in his wigwam and let them do as they pleased with him," he said, "If General Gaines had come with only the regular troops at the Island, he should have remained in his wigwam, but to have done so with men that the officers had no control over would have been sure death

49

to him." In this he acted wisely, as among these volunteers were many frontiersmen who had had friends killed by the Indians, and were prepared to avenge their death on these or any other Indians.

In a few days there was another meeting with Black Hawk, and a treaty concluded, that the Indians should stay on the other side of the river, and the Government would give them as much corn as they could have raised if they had not been disturbed. The Government appointed two men, Mr. Rinnah Wells and myself, to go over their fields and make an estimate of the corn they might have raised. I do not now remember the estimate, but it amounted to several thousand bushels.[17] Thus ended this season's operations. Now commences the more serious part of our story.

In the spring of 1832, notwithstanding the agreement of the Indians to keep on the west side of the river, they came over, breaking their treaty, made only the summer before. They crossed at Burlington, and came up, as usual, with their canoes and horses. As soon

[17] This treaty, concluded with Black Hawk and his followers on June 30, 1831, is printed in full in Stevens, *The Black Hawk War*, 96–97. It contains nothing about supplying the Indians with corn, and this portion of the author's recital is incorrect.

as the Government ascertained this, General Atkinson was sent from Jefferson Barracks with a regiment of men, reaching here before the Indians.[18]

The Indians did not make more than ten miles a day, but came along regularly, reaching here soon after the General, and keeping on the south side of the big island, in Rock River, which I had never known them to do before.

When they were nearly up to where Milan now stands, I crossed the river by fording, to see if I could ascertain their movements. The first Indians I saw were four young men. They had fine looking guns, and seemed to be well armed. One of them was Black Hawk's son, Seoskuk, who was one of the finest looking Indians I ever saw. He was about thirty years of age, and a splendid looking fellow. I asked him where they were going. He answered by saying, "Maybe they should go over to their old village, or they might stop where they were, or go up Rock River to Prophetstown." Seoskuk

[18] General Atkinson reached Fort Armstrong the night of April 12–13, 1832. Black Hawk's band had crossed the Mississippi at Yellow Banks, below the mouth of Rock River, on April 6, and for almost three weeks was engaged in moving slowly northward toward the Winnebago country on Rock River.

51

asked me if there were many soldiers at the
fort. I told him there were a good many. I
was the only white man who had any communication with them at this point. They
finally went up Rock River about two miles
and camped for the night.

The next morning, at the old fort, we could
hear them beating their drums and singing so
plainly that they seemed but a short distance
from us. They were probably five miles distant, and it was quite remarkable, the country being so hilly between them and us, that
we should hear them so distinctly. It is hard
to tell what this demonstration was for. I
have thought it might have been on account
of their passing this point without being mo-
lested by General Atkinson, as they knew
he was at the island with an extra regiment.
This same morning General Atkinson, not
understanding their movements, was anxious to inform the frontier settlers of their
danger, but the only ford on the river was so
near the Indians that it was not thought safe
to make a crossing. I proposed to take the
dispatch to the nearest settlements. To
avoid the Indians I took a canoe and went
down the river until I passed the mouth of
Rock River. Here I took great pains to hide
my canoe, as my getting home depended on
this, and made the rest of my journey on

foot. The dispatch from General Atkinson to the settlers was to this effect, "That there was now no doubt but what we were to have a conflict with the Indians, urging them to take care of themselves, and get out of the way." I had to camp out the first night, and after walking forty miles the next day, reached the settlement. I went to the different settlements, gave the warning of General Atkinson, and returned home. On coming to the river I very fortunately found my canoe where I had hid it, and then came on up to the Island.

We all supposed the General would stop the Indians at this point, but he did not, but called on the Governor for help. He was soon here with 1,800 mounted men. About three hundred men had already rendezvoused at Dixon, and were waiting for orders. All was dependent upon General Atkinson getting ready to follow the Indians up Rock River.

The stream being too shoal for steamboats, they had to resort to the next best thing, the old keelboat, and it was a hard matter to get supplies of them on so short notice. He succeeded in getting one that would carry eighty tons, the largest I ever saw. This boat was manned by seventy regular soldiers; they had another of thirty-five tons, and several Mackinaw boats, also well manned. These were loaded with provisions, and after two hard days' work we got over the rapids of Rock River, and on the eighth of May, started on the war expedition. General Atkinson had several hundred regulars with him, so in manning these boats he changed hands every other day, as it was very laborious work, Rock River being a very rapid stream at that time of the year. Our first camping place was about two miles above the Chicago and Rock Island Railroad Bridge. Our second at the mouth of Canoe Creek, our third at Sand Prairie. This part of the river was so crooked that we made but slow progress. Our fourth encampment was about two miles above Prophetstown. I remember this as though it were yesterday.

The troops were officered by General Atkinson, Colonel Zachary Taylor, afterwards President of the United States, Captain Abraham Lincoln, who filled the same high office, Captain, afterwards Major General, Harney, and other officers. Captain Lincoln belonged to the volunteer forces, and the others to the regulars.[19]

[19] Lincoln served as a captain of Illinois militia in the war, but the bracketing of his name with the regular army officers here mentioned imputes to him an importance wholly out of keeping with the actual situation.

It was about the middle of May, and the moon being full, the night was beautiful. The men were enjoying themselves as I had not seen them before; little thinking that so near them their friends were fleeing for safety, and some were being overtaken and killed. About ten o'clock the next morning we met a young man by the name of Hultz, from Dixon's Ferry, who told us of Major Stillman's defeat by the Indians, and that there was probably a great loss of life. Major Stillman had rendezvoused at Dixon, with about three hundred men that had been raised in the neighborhood of Peoria, while the Governor and his men rendezvoused at Beardstown. The Governor was ordered to this place, and when he reached here Major Stillman had been several days in camp; his men already tired of camp life, Stillman proposed to the Governor, while he was waiting for General Atkinson and the boats, to take his men and go and see where the Indians were.

The Governor consented to their going, and they drew rations for four or five days. According to army regulations at that time, whisky constituted a part of the rations. On the first day out they seemed to conclude they could carry their whisky best by drinking it all in one day, and before night they had very nearly accomplished this task, and a good many of them were not altogether sober. About an hour before sundown they went into camp, within three or four miles of the Indians. They had not been in camp long before Black Hawk sent three of his braves with a flag of truce, saying for Black Hawk, "That it was now night, and for that reason he did not come himself, but that he would come in the morning and talk with them, and did not intend to fight."

Black Hawk sent five of his men out on the prairie to see how their flag was received. About twenty or thirty of our men, being under the influence of whisky, gathered up their horses and guns, and rode out to where these Indians were sitting, apparently unconcerned, not expecting any harm. They allowed our men to come within a few feet of them, when our men, be it said to their shame, deliberately raised their guns, killing three of the Indians, the other two fleeing to their encampment. The Indians who brought the flag of truce, took advantage of the flurry, sprang away and escaped. Now our folks prepared to meet the Indians, as they felt sure of a fight. They mounted, formed in line, and moved slowly towards the Indian encampment. As soon as the

news of the attack on their men reached the
Indians, they flew to arms in the greatest
possible speed, and came on to the fight.
The Indians commenced firing at a long distance, and before many shots had been fired
our men commenced a stampede for Dixon,
the Indians close in the rear, killing all who
were unhorsed in the flight. The horse of
Black Buffalo came into Dixon that night—
he had left the Indians again. The men who
first came into Dixon reported that a large
part of the command had been killed, and it
was not known for some time but that it was
so. A considerable number of the men from
the country about the Illinois River, instead
of coming into Dixon went to their homes.
The next day the Governor sent out a strong
force to bury the dead. They found eleven
whites killed, scattered along for several
miles, and not more than five or six Indians,
including the three killed on the prairie.[20]
There was an Indian living here by the name
of Nahpope, who, before General Gaines
came here, had gone to Malden, in Canada.

[20] In the battle of Stillman's Run on May 14, 1832,
about 40 warriors, led by Black Hawk, put to ignomini-
ous flight eight times their number of Illinois militia.
For Black Hawk's own account of the affair see his *Life*
(Lakeside Classics Ed.), 139–45. Stevens (*Black Hawk
War*, 136–37) argues that the defeat was not due to
drunkenness.

The British part of our Indians made a practice, as well as most of the Indians of the North-west, of going to Canada to pay court to the English. Colonel Davenport told me they would collect in large numbers on the Detroit side of the river, and the authorities at Malden would fix on a particular day for each tribe to cross, and would give them a day's entertainment. They prepared a feast, and met the Indians with a band of music, and escorted them into the fort, where a great deal was done for their pleasure and amusement.[21]

Nahpope and some others had gone to Canada before there was any demonstration, in 1831, to drive them off, and came back in the fall in perfect ignorance of the removal of the Indians.

During the winters of 1831–32 Nahpope continued to run back and forth from our Indians to the Winnebago and Potawatomi, making Black Hawk believe that when

[21] Following the American occupation of Detroit in 1796 the British Government established Fort Malden at the mouth of Detroit River. Here, also was the headquarters of the Indian Superintendent, to whom the Indians for hundreds of miles around periodically resorted to receive their presents and confer with their British "Father." The ruins of Fort Malden may still be seen at Amherstburg, where the Dominion Government maintains a beautiful historical museum.

he got up Rock River these tribes would help him, and when he reached Milwaukee the English would assist him.

When Black Hawk, on his way up Rock River, reached Sycamore Creek, where our army found him, those Indians told him they could not bring themselves into trouble with the Government, and consequently he could not look to them for assistance. After meeting these Indians, I have not the least doubt but Black Hawk intended to give himself and people up without making any resistance, had our men not been intoxicated, and therefore violated his flag of truce. The time was now past for parleying with the Indians. From this time the prospect was war. The Indians now flew to unprotected white settlements, waylaid the roads leading from one point to another, killing a number of people in a few days. There were fifteen killed on Indian Creek. They carried off captive two young ladies by the name of Hall, after killing all the other members of the family except a brother, quite a young boy, who made his escape. These young ladies were afterwards bought by the Potawatomi, who paid for them in horses, and returned them to our government. Their clothes being quite shabby, the ladies of Galena gave them new clothing, and they

were brought to Rock Island on their way to
Morgan County.[22]

They waylaid the roads leading from
Dixon to Galena. At Buffalo Grove a party
of men were passing, unconscious of danger,
as the settlements were too far apart to get
any news so soon of Stillman's defeat. One
of this party was our Indian agent by the
name of Savry, another Thomas Kinney,
and another by the name of Hawley; the
other members of the party I cannot name.
The Indians lay behind a large, long log,
near the road. They fired, killing one man
and one horse, then killing the man who had
lost his horse. Mr. Savry was one of the
killed. Mr. Hawley having a very fine
horse, they followed him in hot pursuit for
thirty miles. After this terrible chase they
ran his horse in marshy ground, and he fell
a victim to their savage rage. Mr. Hawley
was a brother of the late Captain Hawley, of
Pleasant Valley, Scott County, Iowa. This
account was given me by Thomas Kinney, a

---

[22] The Indian Creek Massacre, near Ottawa, occurred
May 20, 1832. Sylvia and Rachel Hall, aged respec-
tively 17 and 15 years, were spared by the Indians and
after a captivity of 12 days were ransomed on June 1.
For the story of the massacre and the experiences of the
Hall girls, see Stevens, *Black Hawk War*, Chap. 21.

neighbor of mine, who was one of the party.[23]

About twenty miles east of Galena, Lieutenant Aubrey, of our old command, started to carry a dispatch from Fort Hamilton a short distance. His horse soon returned with a bloody saddle, and it was evident he had been shot by the Indians. It so happened that old General Dodge, with twenty men, was at the fort, and he started quickly in pursuit. Soon finding the dead man, they followed the trail of the Indians, which by the long grass is easily done. They soon came in sight of them, thirteen in all, on foot. They were making their way in great haste to the Pecatonica bottom, where the grass was from six to eight feet high. The General dismounted, detailing every fourth man to hold the horses, leaving fifteen men to pursue the Indians. They followed the

[23] "Savry" was Felix St. Vrain, Indian agent at Fort Armstrong. Since Spencer knew him, the spelling "Savry" evidently represents the settlers' way of pronouncing his name. St. Vrain and six settlers, en route for Galena, were attacked near Buffalo Grove on May 24 by about thirty Sauk. St. Vrain and three of his companions were slain, the remaining three escaped. The body of Hawley was never found, and our author's story of his fate is perhaps as accurate as any. St. Vrain was a cultivated man and a sincere friend of the Indians. See Stevens, *Black Hawk War*, 169–71.

trail almost to the river, when suddenly the Indians sprang up and fired upon them, killing two of our men, one of these being Samuel Wells, a son of Rinnah Wells, and a member of our old company. Our men returned their fire, bringing down eleven of the Indians the first fire, the remaining two taking refuge in the river, trying to make their escape. Our men, reloading their guns, fired, killing them in the water, thus securing the thirteen.[24]

[24] Some confusion, either of memory, or otherwise, is apparent in the author's narrative of the Pecatonica battle, concerning which Thwaites states (*Wis. Hist. Colls.*, XII, 243) that "the details of no event in the entire war have been so thoroughly discussed and quarreled over." William Aubrey of Mound Fort (not Griffith Aubrey of the Rock River Rangers, with whom our author has confused him) was killed on June 6. Stevens, *Black Hawk War*, 180–82. The man killed near Fort Hamilton on the morning of June 16 was Henry Appel. Gen. Dodge led a party of 29 men in pursuit of the Indians, who, 17 in number, took refuge in the swampy lowland of a bend of the Pecatonica River. In the brief battle all the Indians were slain by Dodge and 17 of his men, various detachments from the total number having been made by the leader before the fight began. Three of the whites (one of them Samuel Wells) were killed, and 2 more were wounded. Dodge's achievement, sufficiently striking in itself, still lives in the local memory, in which, with the passage of time and much retelling, its significance has been considerably exaggerated. An historical monument erected in 1922 affirms that "The annals of Indian warfare offer no parallel to this battle."

About eight or ten miles north of Galena, where two men were at work in a corn field, one plowing, the other hoeing corn, two Indians placed themselves so that the man plowing would come near them, killing him the first fire. The other, seeing his companion shot down, and having no means of defense, took to his heels for Galena. The Indians pursued him several miles, but, being a swift runner, he made his escape. The Indians returned to the house, taking what suited their fancy.

There was a large canoe at the house, and it being too heavy for them to get to the river, they found a cross-cut saw in the house, and cut off as much as would ferry them over the river, and made good their escape.

Some twenty miles south-east from Galena, where Elizabeth now is, there was a small settlement of miners, who had erected a rude fort for their protection. An old man by the name of Dixon, who was a frontiersman, and well accustomed to Indians, started for Dixon's Ferry, accompanied by a man on foot. About a mile from the place of starting they met a large force of Indians, who fired on them, wounding the man on foot. The country being rough and wooded, Dixon, by his dexterity, riding about rapidly, showing himself in many different places in a short time, gave the Indians to believe they had a large force of armed and mounted men to contend with. In this way Dixon gave the wounded man time to reach the fort and apprise the settlers of their danger. The people had scattered out about their business, but the alarm being given they were immediately collected in the fort. If it had not been for Dixon's ingenious maneuvering, detaining the Indians, they must have been all massacred, as they had hardly time to reach the fort before the Indians took possession of the village and surrounded the fort. The Indians could go from one house to another with comparative safety. They plundered the houses of whatever suited their fancy, and carried off all the valuables, as well as most of the provisions, in the village. Watching about the fort, if any one showed himself inside he was fired on by them. One man, showing his head above the fort, received a bullet, breaking his neck. Dixon, instead of stopping at the fort, pressed on to Galena to get a force for their relief. They came on as rapidly as possible, and, when a short distance south of Elizabeth, they found a large force of Indians secreted in the bushes and grass. The Indians, allowing our men to come within a few feet of them, fired, killing several, among others Mr. George Ames, a brother of Mrs. William Brooks, Sr.[25]

About this time there were about seventy regular soldiers stationed at Kellogg's Grove, there being a large hewed log house there which made a safe rendezvous for persons going from one point to another, or for those hard pressed by the Indians, which was often the case. One of our mounted companies was driven in by the Indians, and was obliged to flee to this place for safety. Hitching their horses as near the house as possible, so as to be able to protect them somewhat from the Indians, they took shelter in the house. The Indians crept up among the trees and shot down fifty-seven horses. They saw one horse acting very strangely, and thought they could see something in the weeds in front of him. They concluded this was an Indian, and so three or four shots were fired at him. After the Indians had left, in looking

[25] Charles Eames (the correct name, according to Stevens, *Black Hawk War*, 184) was killed June 18 in a fight with 7 Indians, in which the whites were worsted and 3 men slain. The attack upon Apple River Fort, at present-day Elizabeth, in which Frederick Dixon (not to be confused with the better-known John Dixon) figured, occurred on June 24. See Stevens, *Black Hawk War*, 184–87, for a better and more accurate account of this affair.

over the battle-field, some of the men from this neighborhood recognized Black Buffalo as the man who was in the weeds. Trading horses had brought him to his death, as he had lost his horse at Stillman's defeat and was trying to get another. He had a long stick with which he hooked the bridle off the stake of the fence, and was trying to creep along and lead him away, but the horse being afraid of him caused our men to discover and kill him.[26]

About this time a company of about forty men stopped at Kellogg's Grove and struck their tents for the night. It being a rainy night,[27] one of the sentinels took shelter near the body of a large tree. Very unexpectedly an Indian put his hand on his shoulder, which was as great a surprise to the Indian as to the soldier. The soldier fired his gun straight up in the air, and our folks, hearing

[26] The author's account of the fight at Kellogg's Grove, on June 25, is both incomplete and inaccurate. There were no regulars present, the soldiers involved being Major John Dement's battalion of Illinois militia. Dement was a capable and spirited leader whose conduct elicited high praise from Black Hawk. See his *Life* (Lakeside Classics Ed.), 150. His followers displayed as little discipline as had the followers of Stillman in the fiasco of Stillman's Run. A good account of the affair is in Stevens, *Black Hawk War*, 197–201.

[27] The night of June 15–16, 1832.

the report, supposed they were attacked by the Indians, and left their tents and went into the house for safety. My brother, R. H. Spencer and four others, were not awakened by the firing, and slept in the tent until morning. The Indians had been prowling around in search of horses, and early in the morning our men got on their trail; the grass being wet they could easily follow it on a fast trot. In about ten miles they came in sight of the Indians. There were only four of them, and they made a signal to give themselves up. But old General Whiteside, who had fought against the Indians in 1812, and for whom Whiteside County was named, showed them that they must fight. The Indians ran into a deep ravine where the water had gullied a large hole, and in this they took shelter. The situation was such that the folks had to get very near in order to see the Indians. This they did by taking advantage of the large trees, which were a good protection. Behind one tree were three or four men, when one of them, a large man, stepped out and said, "Let me give them a pop," and fired, and in return received two bullets through his body. General Whiteside now said: "Boys, rush on them—their guns are empty." They closed upon them, killing them all. They now started on their return, four men carrying the wounded man, taking turns. After traveling several miles they were attacked by a superior force of the enemy, and in turn had to flee for safety. General Whiteside tried hard to make a stand with fifteen or twenty men, to check the Indians for a few minutes, but could not succeed, and the men who were carrying the wounded man came near being left to the mercy of the Indians, as the men detailed to hold their horses, only thinking of themselves, were riding away, leading their horses with them. While they were mounting their horses, my brother saw an Indian on a white horse thrust a long spear into the wounded man, whom they were obliged to leave on the ground. The next man who came along, with his tomahawk cut off the wounded man's head. In this attack the Indians killed two of our men besides the one at first wounded.[28]

During the trouble with the Indians, there was an old man, who in his religious belief was a Dunkard, who started from the frontier settlement about LaSalle, to go to Chicago, about a hundred miles distant. His

[28] The white leader in this affair was not General Whiteside, as the author mistakenly supposes, but Captain Adam Snyder. A good account of it is in Stevens, *Black Hawk War*, 176–79.

friends did all they could to dissuade him from going, as he must make the journey on horseback and alone. But he was determined to go, feeling that he would not be disturbed in the journey; that an overruling power would protect him against the Indians. After leaving the settlement, when a few miles on his way, he was discovered by a band of Indians. On coming up with them, he permitted them to come within a few yards of him without showing the least fear. This sect, unlike people of his time, wore their beards long and full, and the Indians had never seen any one with a long beard before. From his strange look or behavior, they were awe-struck, and debated among themselves what was best to do with the old man. The old man had a very fine horse, which seemed to decide the question, and so, after following along with him for some time, they killed him. On their return to camp that night, they found some Potawatomi in their camp, and told them they had killed the Devil that day, exhibiting the scalp as it had been taken off, with the beard attached.[29]

---

[29] Rev. Adam Payne, whose killing is here narrated, was set upon by 3 Indians while en route from Plainfield to Ottawa, shortly after the Indian Creek Massacre of May 20. For a somewhat different account of the killing of Payne see Stevens, *Black Hawk War*, 167-68.

The Indians were now forced to take a position on the upper part of Rock River, occupying the country from Lake Koshkonong to where Whitewater now stands. This being wooded country, it was very difficult to drive them out.

After fighting and skirmishing with them from the middle of May until the last of July, they finally got them started for the Mississippi. The Indians now made all possible haste for Iowa, our army pursuing them closely, overtook them near the Wisconsin River. On the bluff, about five miles from the river, the Indians made their stand, and fought one of the hardest battles of the war. The Indians were found in the high grass, and by taking advantage of their hiding place, would load their guns, rise up and fire, then drop down again and load. They left more than forty dead on the ground, and our army, as they followed them up, found their dead scattered for several days. It was believed they lost more than eighty, who were killed, or died from their wounds. This battle was fought by the Indians to give time to get their families across the Wisconsin River.[30] Here they very hastily made

[30] This was the battle of Wisconsin Heights, fought July 21, 1832, about 25 miles northwest of Madison. The author's report of the Indian loss is necessarily

bark canoes, taking the bark from large elm
trees. Cutting the bark eight or ten feet
long, they shaved the ends, making it thin
and pliable, so they could tie it together, and
in this way keep the water out. This is not
the way of making a regular bark canoe, but
a very good substitute.

In these rude canoes ninety women and
children, and one old man, came down the
river to its mouth, where they were inter-
cepted by our people, and brought to Rock
Island and held as prisoners.[31]

Our army was detained at the Wisconsin
River several days in crossing. It being a
very rapid stream it was difficult to cross,
and as there were no boats, they took an old
hewed log house and made a raft or rafts,
and finally succeeded in crossing.

inaccurate and probably much exaggerated. Black
Hawk states that he lost 6 men. *Life*, 154. At near-by
Fort Winnebago, the contemporary report of the battle
stated 50 Indians had been killed, with a white loss of
1 killed and 8 wounded. See Mrs. John H. Kinzie,
Wau-Bun, the Lakeside Classics volume for 1932,
p. 509.

[31] The author's statement is much too creditable to
the humanity of the whites. Instead of being held as
prisoners, all but half a score of these noncombatants
were slaughtered, drowned, or perished from starvation.
See Thwaites, "Story of the Black Hawk War," in *Wis.
Hist. Colls.*, XII, 254–55; Mrs. Kinzie, *Wau-Bun*
(Lakeside Classics Ed.), 516–17.

While making preparations to cross the river, one night, after the Indians had all left, there came an Indian in the night, and standing on a high point on the opposite side from our army, with a very powerful voice, which could be distinctly understood, said, "If the whites would let the Indians go they would go back to Iowa, and remain quiet and peaceable." But our army was now anxious to punish them, and so hastened across the river, took their trail, which brought them to the Mississippi.[32] They found, at all the camping places of the Indians, skeletons of their horses, as they were now reduced to this kind of food, having no time to hunt, pressing with all their energy to reach the Mississippi, before our army should overtake and destroy them. But after all their exertions, their great suffering from hunger and exhaustion, they were doomed to disappointment. They had succeeded in reaching the river, and had safely crossed many of their women and children, before our army came up.

[32] This appeal of Nahpope, Black Hawk's second in command of the Indians, was made in the night of July 21–22, following the battle of Wisconsin Heights. According to Thwaites, it was uttered in the Winnebago tongue, which no one in the camp of the white army could understand, for which reason it received no consideration. See *Wis. Hist. Colls.*, XII, 255.

Here at the river was fought the second hard battle, killing one hundred and fifty of the Indians, and some of their women and children, they being huddled together in the high weeds and grass.[33] One can get some idea of their great hunger from a little circumstance that happened there. It became necessary to amputate the arm of a little girl about ten years old. Some one gave her a biscuit, which she continued to eat during the operation.

During the trouble with the Indians, the government brought down a band of one hundred and fifty Sioux, who were the most dreaded enemy our Indians had, on account of their great numbers. They quartered them at Galena, and tried to get them in the contest, but did not succeed, they being too cowardly to attack the Sauk and Foxes when they were armed, and they quietly slipped away in the night.

Now I have the most unpleasant part of my story to tell. After the Indians had crossed the river, and were almost defense-

[33] The battle, or more properly the massacre, of the Bad Axe, August 2, 1832. About 150 Indians were killed and as many more drowned while vainly attempting to escape their pursuers by plunging into the Mississippi. For a good account of the affair see Thwaites, "Story of the Black Hawk War," in *Wis. Hist. Colls.*, XII, 257-60.

less, having lost almost all their guns and ammunition in crossing the river, our army put a band of these merciless Sioux on their trail, who, knowing how perfectly helpless they were, were glad of the opportunity to destroy them. I will give the account of this terrible massacre as given by a squaw, who had lived with a white man by the name of Nathan Smith. I knew them both well.

She said her brother, by the name of Wishita, a fine looking man, and a chief of considerable standing, was wounded while crossing the Mississippi, but he, with great exertion, reached the western shore. Here the bank being steep, she tried to get him out, but could not succeed, and was obliged to leave him behind her on account of her company, which was already in advance of her.

She had crossed the river on a pony, carrying her child, about a year old, before her. They hurried on, fearing an attack of our army, or an attack of the Sioux, as they were now in their country. They had traveled that day and night, and until the latter part of the next day, without food, when they succeeded in killing some game, and camped for the night. That night, they, for the first time in many weary days and nights, had plenty to eat. They had camped in a valley, and the morning was very foggy. They had eaten an early breakfast, and were about starting on their journey, she just mounting her horse, when the Sioux, with a great noise, whooping and yelling, broke into their camp, killing large numbers of them regardless of age or sex.

She rode off as fast as her horse could possibly go, carrying her child before her. She said the motion of her horse was so hard on her child, she thought for some time it was dead, and looked for some thick bush or weeds that she could throw it in to hide it from the Sioux.

She knew by keeping a southern course it would bring her to her friends.

After traveling more than two hundred miles without another human being save her child, without food, and expecting hourly to be overtaken by her enemies, she at last found a trail where Keokuk had been out on a buffalo hunt. Following this trail, it brought her to the Indian village on the Iowa River.

This last battle fought on the Mississippi, was the noted battle of Bad Axe, and Black Hawk, feeling that he and his people were thoroughly overcome, did not cross the river, but went up the river and gave himself up to the Winnebago, who brought him a prisoner to Prairie du Chien. Black Hawk's son,

Seoskuk, Nahpope, Pashphaw, the Stabbing Chief, and several of the principal men, accompanied him to prison. They were sent to Washington about the latter part of the summer, where they remained until the next spring, when they were set at liberty and started on their return home, passing through New York City. President Jackson and a party of friends happened to be with Black Hawk on their way to New York, and General Jackson's friends complained that the Indians diverted the attention of the people too much from the President.[34]

There was a great demonstration in New York at that time, and the Indians received much attention. Many of the ladies kissed Seoskuk, which was a matter of little comment, as one rarely meets so fine a specimen of humanity in a life-time. The ladies took their rings off from their fingers and gave them to the Indians. Black Hawk showed me some of the rings, and said he had fifty just as fine.

From New York they went by the canal to Buffalo, through the lakes to Green Bay, up

[34] Black Hawk was confined at Jefferson Barracks, near St. Louis, throughout the autumn and winter of 1832–33. He was sent upon his eastern tour in the spring of 1833, when he was briefly confined at Fortress Monroe from April 26 to June 4. The encounter with President Jackson to which the author refers was at a theater in Baltimore the evening of June 6.

the Fox River, down the Wisconsin to its mouth, and down the Mississippi to Rock Island. Here, fortunately, I happened to meet Black Hawk, and he was unusually talkative. He told me of their trip to Washington, of the crowds of people they saw in New York, and showed me some of the many presents he had received on the journey. He told me of the great wonder of seeing a man go up in a balloon. He said the man had a great knife in his hand (meaning a sword), which he waved back and forth, and then he went up, up, up, and looking and pointing up, he said, "Panoche! panoche!" meaning a great way off. He was in good spirits, expecting to reach his family the next day.

Major Garland, of the army, under whose charge they had traveled, being instructed to secure a kind reception for them from their nation, sent a messenger to advise Keokuk of their arrival. Keokuk was encamped on the Iowa shore of the river, about twenty miles below, and although Black Hawk and his party were his enemies, he determined to give them a respectful and cordial reception. A message was returned to that effect, and at noon the following day the dull sound of the Indian drum proclaimed the approach of the chief. He, with his three wives, in two canoes lashed together with a canopy over them, followed by many of his braves, came up the river to the foot of the Island, and then landed on the right bank, where they remained painting and dressing themselves for some time.

Keokuk, followed by his braves, crossed the river, and before coming to Black Hawk's camp, said to them: "The Great Spirit has sent our brothers back; let us shake hands in friendship." On reaching the spot where Black Hawk and his friends were encamped, they found them seated in front of their tent, silent and motionless—doubtful, perhaps, of the reception that would be given them. Keokuk extended his hand to Black Hawk, and then to the rest of his party, without speaking, his followers imitating his example, and then the whole company seated themselves on the ground. No one spoke, each waiting until the chief should break the silence. After about fifteen minutes, Keokuk asked Black Hawk how long he had been on the way, adding that he had been expecting him, and was on his way to meet him when he heard of his arrival. The next day, in the council, Black Hawk thanked Major Garland for his kindness. He said: "I and my son, and all our party, thank our Great Father for what he has done. He is old, I am old; we shall soon go to the Great Spirit, and be at rest. He sent us through his great villages. We saw many white men, and were kindly treated. We thank them—say to them we thank them. We thank you for traveling with us. Your path was long and crooked. We never saw so many white men before; but when with you we felt as safe as if among friends. When you come to the Mississippi again you shall come to my lodges; now I have none. On your road home you will pass where our village once was. No one lives there now—all are gone. I give you my hand; we may never meet again, but we shall remember you. The Great Spirit will be with you and your wives and children. I will shake hands with my brethren here, and then I am done." Black Hawk thanked Keokuk and his nation for their attention to his wife and children, as they had given them shelter when they had none, and had protected them while he was far away. He felt happy to have escaped with so slight punishment, as when he gave himself up he hardly knew what would be the result. It must have been quite humiliating to the old man to have to yield up all his rights as head of the nation to a young man like Keokuk. Sad must have been his heart when he said, "I will listen to Keokuk. I will soon be far away, where I shall have no village, no band—I shall be alone." Still, we must admire the generous course Keokuk pursued with him, when, in after years, they took a trip together, taking in their course all the principal eastern cities.

They, with other Indians, were sitting in council in the presence of the Secretary of War, when Keokuk arose and said: "There is one here who does not belong to the council, but he has been accustomed to sit with us at home, and is our friend; we have brought him here with us, and hope he will be welcome."

Black Hawk lived until the year 1838, when he died on the third of October at his village on the Des Moines River, and his body was disposed of, at his special request, after the manner of the chiefs of his tribe. He was placed upon the ground in a sitting posture, his hands grasping his cane. They usually made a shallow hole in the ground, setting the body in up to the waist, so that most of the body was above ground. The part above ground was then covered by a buffalo robe, and a trench about eight feet square was dug about the grave. In this trench they set picketing about eight feet high, which secured the grave against wild animals. Not long after Black Hawk died, some one, more troubled with phrenology than reverence, took his head and carried it away, which so distressed his family that his sons came into Burlington to Governor Lucas, who was then Governor of the Territory of Iowa, to see if the Government would not have it restored to them. But they did not succeed in getting it.[35]

When I first came here there were quite a number of these high picketings still standing, where their chiefs had been buried, and the body of a chief was disposed of in this way while I lived near their village. The common mode of burial was to dig a shallow grave, wrap the body in a blanket, place it in the grave, and fill it nearly full of dirt; then take split sticks about three feet long and stand them in the grave so that their tops would come together in the form of a roof; then they filled in more earth so as to hold the sticks in place. I saw a father and mother start out alone to bury their child,

[35] On the desecration of Black Hawk's remains see Stevens, *The Black Hawk War*, 273-74. Instead of the head, the entire body was stolen by a Dr. Turner of near-by Van Buren County, and sent to St. Louis, where the skeleton was cleaned and articulated. Governor Lucas of Iowa Territory, on learning of the desecration took possession of the skeleton, subsequently depositing it with the Burlington Geological and Historical Society, where it remained until consumed in a fire in 1855.

about a year old. They carried it by tying it
up in a blanket, and putting a long stick
through the blanket, each taking an end of
the stick. I have also seen the dead bodies
placed in trees. This is done by digging a
trough out of a log, placing the body in it and
covering it. I have seen several bodies in one
tree. I think when they are disposed of in
this way it is by special request, as I knew of
an Indian woman who lived with a white
family, who desired her body placed in a
tree, which was accordingly done. Doubtless there was some particular superstition
attached to this mode, though I do not remember to have heard what it was.

Our nearest neighbor, living fifty miles
south-east from here, on the old mining road
leading from Beardstown to Galena, where
the road crossed Henderson River, was an
old man by the name of Atwood, an English-
man by birth. I do not consider him a fair
representative of an Old Settler, but as many
who lived here in early times have come in
contact with him I cannot forbear to give
him a passing notice. He said he was a lord
in England, and when he took ship for America great crowds of people gathered to see
him safely started. His fame had reached
New York in advance of his arrival, and
large numbers were gathered kneeling on the

shore to receive him. He told them to stand up, as he was only a man. Mr. Atwood's settlement there was a year or two before ours here, so we had occasion to do some trading with him in his farm products. After a few months' traffic with him he sent us word that he had all the paper money he could secrete, and, as paper money was liable to be stolen or burned up, if we continued to trade with him we would have to bring either gold or silver, which he could bury in the ground. In stopping with him he told me of a remarkable cure he had performed upon a man where gangrene had set in. Among a great many eminent physicians who had visited this man and given him up as incurable, was Dr. Franklin. I said to him that I did not know that Dr. Franklin practiced medicine. His wife spoke up and said: "Yes he did, all through North Carolina, where I lived." I asked the old man how many hogs he had. He hesitated some time, and began to make excuses. His hogs "had strayed away and were lost— the Indians had killed a good many—and now he only had about seven hundred left." There were not seven hundred hogs within twenty miles of him. One of his neighbors by the name of McGee, a blacksmith, was at work in his shop at a very difficult job. Being a good deal plagued with his work, the old man came in and began telling some of his long yarns, when McGee stopped his work, and addressed the old man in this way: "I make it a practice to believe some men because they tell the truth, others to accommodate them, but," bringing out an oath, said, "I won't believe you upon any consideration." He said he was not troubled again for a long time with the old man. His neighbors said they had calculated the time it would take to do the different things he had done, and the different places he had lived, and the number of years he had stayed in each place, and ascertained he was over a thousand years old, being the oldest man we have any record of.

I now feel it not only a duty, but a great pleasure, to make some mention of the old settlers of Rock Island County. I came to the State at such an early day, and traveled over it so extensively, making my home at two different times in very new parts of the State, that I had a great opportunity of judging of frontier life, and of frontier men. Of all my knowledge of the settlement of the State, our old settlers were the most intelligent and best informed of any who came under my notice. There have been some statements made about us, which have had a large circulation, in regard to our abusing the Indians, and whipping their women, which are basely false, or if not, never came under my notice. Our relation to the Indians, after the first summer, was very peculiar. We having had a good title to our lands from the Government, felt we were entitled to be protected in our rights, while the Indians claimed the lands to be theirs with just as much assurance. Under such conflicting circumstances, losing the greater part of our crops, being compelled, a part of the time, to stay in the fort for safety, we lived almost three seasons together without any serious outbreak among us, which seems to me to be flattering to both whites and Indians. I feel that the Old Settlers of Rock Island County are very nearly related to me. Our privations and hardships brought us very near to each other, and I cannot but sympathize in the sorrows of each Old Settler, and rejoice in their well doing.

Fifty Years
in Iowa

J. M. D. BURROWS.

R. M. PRETTYMAN.

FIFTY YEARS IN IOWA:

BEING THE

PERSONAL REMINISCENCES OF
J. M. D. BURROWS,

CONCERNING THE

MEN AND EVENTS, SOCIAL LIFE, INDUSTRIAL
INTERESTS, PHYSICAL DEVELOPMENT,
AND COMMERCIAL PROGRESS

OF

DAVENPORT AND SCOTT COUNTY,

DURING THE PERIOD
FROM

1838 TO 1888.

DAVENPORT, IOWA:
GLASS & COMPANY, PRINTERS AND BINDERS.
1888.

Explanatory

IN submitting to my fellow-citizens this volume, containing the recollections of a round half century of life in Iowa, and more particularly in Davenport and Scott County, among the old-time friends and their descendants, to whom I now look for such audience as I may be favored with, it seems proper for me to explain briefly the circumstances that have led me to attempt a task so unaccustomed as the making of a book.

About a year ago, after a long life of constant activity and exceptionally good health, I was stricken with heart disease. As usual with that dreaded malady, the attack, in my case, was wholly unheralded and unexpected. It prostrated me completely at the time, and since then I have been unable to perform any physical labor.

Casting about, in this extremity, what I should do to gain a livelihood while life might be granted to me yet a little longer, it was suggested by friends that many persons would read with interest some account of men and events in Scott County, as I knew

them, during the pioneer days of the early
'40's, together with such personal gossip and
reminiscences of business struggles, social
changes, and other local matters in the later
history of Davenport, as I could set down in
narrative form.

Acting on this idea, I have written the
book presented herewith. Much of the writing has been done when the writer was able
barely to sit up in bed. Many of the facts
have been jotted down regardless of tempo-
ral sequence, as they came uppermost in my
mind, between spells of physical suffering.
The exigency of the circumstances, forcing
me into the heretofore untried field of litera-
ture, even in this humble form, must stand
as my apology for whatever is crude in the
story.

One feature of the book does not please
me, as I read the proofs of the completed
work: it is that the narrative seems so per-
meated with the presence of J. M. D. Burrows. Many times his personality has crept
in almost without the knowledge, certainly
without the intent, of the writer. These in-
stances, which escaped notice while the history was being written, are unpleasantly
apparent to me now. But, as I have been
giving my own recollections, mostly of scenes
in which I was a principal actor, I hope that

my friends will consider these repeated, though oftentimes unconscious, references to self as, at the worst, a necessary evil, rather than as purposely intrusive egotism.

The more confidential relationship of reader and writer in prefatory chapters must be my excuse for one more purely personal statement. Every one who knows anything of me and my history, knows that I made several fortunes during my active business career in Davenport. Some may ask, and with reason, "Why did he not lay by a competency against the barren days of old age?" I answer that it was my hope and expectation to do so; yet, in the years when prosperity smiled upon me, there were crises in the commercial life of Davenport and Scott County, when the welfare of the community seemed to demand my continuance in business. I continued, and sacrificed more than one fortune in my perhaps mistaken, but at least unselfish, loyalty to the interests of the community. Had the right man appeared to take my place at any one of several important junctures in the affairs of Davenport, I should have stepped down and out gladly. As it was, I stood in the breach too long.

To this closing explanation, I add the hope that this work—my last—will prove not only interesting to such of my friends and former

Explanatory

co-workers as still live to read it, but instructive to the younger generation, as a faithful, if rudely drawn, chronicle of the vicissitudes which we, who are passing rapidly away and out of their memories, underwent to make Davenport what it is.

J. M. D. B.

Table of Contents

Table of Contents

Table of Contents

99

Table of Contents

Table of Contents

Table of Contents

Table of Contents

Table of Contents

Fifty Years in Iowa

Chapter 1

The Villages of Stephenson and Davenport in 1838.—A
First Glimpse of Iowa Scenery.—The Ferry Primeval
and Captain John Wilson.—Citizens, 25 Cents;
Strangers, 50 Cents.—From Cincinnati by Horse
and Buggy.—Hardships on the Way.—Some Early
Settlers.

ON the 27th day of July, 1838, I was on
board the magnificent steamer *Brazil*, Captain Orrin Smith, my destination being Stephenson, now Rock Island
City, Illinois.[1] When I arose in the morning,
the steamer was just landing at Buffalo,
Scott County, Wisconsin Territory, now
Iowa.[2] The scene upon which I gazed en-

[1] Rock Island County was created by legislative
action in 1833, and the county seat was fixed at Far-
numsburg on the site of present-day Rock Island. In
1835 the adjoining town of Stephenson was platted and
made the county seat. In March, 1841 it was incorporated and renamed Rock Island City.

[2] Wisconsin Territory, organized July 4, 1836, in-
cluded all of present-day Iowa, Minnesota, and the
eastern half of the Dakotas. On July 4, 1838, Wisconsin
Territory was reduced to the limits of the present state

chanted me. The sloping lawns and wooded bluffs, with the sea of beautiful wild flowers, were a picture of loveliness such as I never had beheld before. The remainder of the trip I spent on the guards of the boat, enraptured with the beauty of the ever-changing scenery.

We arrived early in the day at the village of Stephenson. Before night my business was accomplished. My landlord, of the Rock Island House, informed me that I would not be able to get a boat until the return of the *Brazil*, some two days later. I will say here, that the Rock Island House was a credit to the town, and a much better hotel than I expected to find in this then new country.

On the next day, after partaking of a good breakfast, I decided to cross the river and examine the lovely little hamlet of about a dozen houses, which looked so cosy, nestled under the bluff. At that time, the ferry was run by that veteran, Captain John Wilson, and consisted of two steamboat yawls and a flat-boat. There were several passengers besides myself, and, as soon as we left the shore, the old gentleman began to collect his fares. I noticed that each passenger paid twenty-

of Wisconsin, the remaining area lying west of the Mississippi being organized as Iowa Territory.

five cents. I tendered my quarter, when I was informed my fare was fifty cents. I demurred, of course, and was surprised, as well as somewhat amused, to be told that for citizens the fare was twenty-five cents, but for strangers it was fifty cents. I replied, "Oh! that is the way you do here, is it? Where I came from, they treat strangers the best."

On landing, I found a beautiful little hamlet of fifteen houses, with a population of about one hundred and fifty persons. I did not expect to see any one that I had ever seen before, but I soon met a man whom I had known well in Cincinnati—a carpenter —B. F. Coates. He received me warmly, and introduced me to D. C. Eldridge and several more Cincinnatians. The little town was settled mostly by people from Cincinnati.[3] They all insisted that I should close up my business in Stephenson, and wait in Davenport until my boat returned, and they would spend the time in showing me the

[3] The site of Davenport had been acquired by Antoine Le Claire, who in 1835 sold it to a company organized for the purpose of laying out a town. This was done in the spring of 1836 and a two-day sale of town lots was held in May. Although a hotel was erected by two of the proprietors this same year, the town grew but slowly. The natural beauty of the site is not exaggerated by our author.

most beautiful country the sun ever shone upon. I consented, and Mr. Coates took a horse and buggy, and drove with me out some five or six miles in different directions.

It was just the time of year when the country showed to best advantage. The prairies were covered with wild flowers, and the beautiful landscape was unsurpassed. I said to myself, "This shall be my home."

On the return of the *Brazil*, I left, with the intention, if I possibly could, to emigrate. As soon as I returned to Cincinnati, I advertised my place for sale, and, in a few weeks, found a purchaser. I then determined to return immediately, and to make a more thorough examination of the country before taking such an important step.

Both the Ohio and Mississippi rivers were, at that time (October), very low, and navigation tedious. I decided to make the trip by land, so purchased a horse and buggy, and was making arrangements for the journey, when I was called upon by John Owens,[4] whom I had never seen before. After intro-

[4] John Owens was born in Wales in 1793 and was brought to New York City in infancy. He served in the War of 1812, and at its close removed with his parents to Cincinnati, where he lived until the migration to Iowa which our author describes. Owens conducted a store in Davenport more than thirty years. He died there, Sept. 27, 1874.

ducing himself, he said he understood I intended to make a trip to Wisconsin Territory, and he wanted to go along. He offered to take a half interest in the outfit. He was not quite ready to go, and I agreed to wait ten days for him.

At last the day arrived, and lo! it was a Friday. Owens said he would not begin such an important enterprise on Friday, and insisted that we should wait until Saturday, which I opposed, on the ground that it was too late in the week. We were both anxious to be off, so we agreed to start on Thursday evening, and go two or three miles, which we did, setting out about sundown, and driving some three miles.

We found the roads through Indiana very rough and tedious, a great share of them being what was called "corduroy"[5] but through Illinois they were excellent, although there was a great want of bridges, and in fording some streams we found it quite dangerous.

The great prairies of Illinois were a magnificent sight—one vast sea of grass and

[5] Corduroy roads were made across low or swampy places by laying sections of tree trunks close together at right angles to the road. The discomforts and difficulties of travel over such a highway remained permanently engraved upon the memories of the pioneers.

flowers, and most of them as level as a floor. We passed very few farms. Fifty years ago there were not many settlements in Illinois. We crossed a number of prairies, where, as might be said, we were out of sight of land—not a house or a tree to be seen. There was a great deal of sickness on our route. We had to attend our own horse, and, most of the time, sleep on the floor, with a blanket and a pillow for our bed.

Ten days and a half from the time we left Cincinnati, we forded Rock River, and soon reached our future home. At that time, Stephenson, on the Illinois side of the Mississippi, was a considerable town, and a much older and more important place than Davenport. Rock Island contained no inhabitants except Colonel George Davenport and his family. Old Fort Armstrong, with its block-houses, occupied the west end of the Island.[6]

Mr. Owens and myself spent some three weeks in thoroughly examining the country. One of the best settlements was in Pleasant Valley. The Hydes, Captain Hawley, Moss

[6] Fort Armstrong, at the foot of Rock Island, was one of a chain of frontier forts established, or re-established, following the War of 1812. It was begun in the spring of 1816 and completed the following year. The garrison was withdrawn and the fort abandoned in 1836.

& Bradley, Sam. Hedges, C. Rowe, Adam Donaldson, the Henleys and Fennos were there. There was a small saw-mill on Duck Creek, and a grist-mill, containing one small run of stone, on Crow Creek. Both these streams contained twice as much water then as now.

We drove back to Allen's Grove; also to Walnut and Hickory Groves, where we found John Dunn, L. Lathrop, Dennis R. Fuller, and the Carters, all of whom were hard at work making themselves homes. Below Rockingham, Enoch Mead, David Sullivan, Captain James Murray, Foster Campbell, James E. Burnsides, Lewis W. Clark, and others, were busily engaged in laying the foundation of Scott County's future prosperity.

Chapter 2

Buying a Squatter's Claim in Scott County.—Cuts
Drawn for Choice of Halves.—The Difficulties of
House-Building.—Down River in a Yawl.—Trials of
Early Navigation.—An Honest Landlady.—A Rail-
road Journey to New Jersey.

AFTER a thorough examination of the
country, and making the acquaintance of many of the settlers, we both
determined to emigrate, and purchased the
eighty-acre tract west of and adjoining the
town. It was a squatter's claim.[7] We paid
four hundred and fifty dollars for it, and
each wanted it, so we agreed to divide it, and
to draw cuts for the first choice. I won, and
chose the half next to the town, for which I
paid two hundred and fifty dollars, Mr.
Owens taking the other half at two hundred
dollars. We then concluded to lay claim to a

[7] In advance of the U. S. survey and sale of the land,
individuals frequently occupied or "squatted" upon
choice tracts. Although they had no legal title to the
tract thus occupied, local public opinion commonly
upheld their claim to it, and newcomers ordinarily first
bought out the squatter before completing title by pur-
chasing the land from the Government. The present
Editor's grandparents thus purchased a Squatter's
claim on migrating to Iowa in 1854.

section of land, and selected Section 17. We divided it, north and south, and, each again wanting the half adjoining the town, we drew cuts, as before. I won, and took the part I wanted.

Fearing we would have trouble to find our claim, we hired Strong Burnell, who was breaking prairie in the vicinity, to plow three furrows around the whole section, for which we paid thirty dollars—ten dollars a furrow. We proposed to plant this strip of plowed ground with locust trees.

The next thing I did, was to make arrangements to build a house on my forty acres. I found a man in Davenport, a settler of that year, who had bought a lot and erected a frame on it, but who had become discouraged, and wished to return East. I bought the frame standing, paying one hundred and twenty-five dollars for it, and engaged B. F. Coates to take it to pieces and put it up on my land, leaving money with him with which to buy weatherboarding, sheathing, etc., and it was agreed that I should bring the shingles, flooring, doors and windows with me in the spring, from Cincinnati, which would be much cheaper and better.

We had now spent three weeks here, by which time we both had become homesick, and began to look around for a way to return, as we did not wish to return by land. I paid Mr. Owens for his interest in the horse and buggy, and let a man have the use of it for keeping it until spring.

The river was so low and the season so late that we could not get a boat, so we bought a yawl of the ferryman, paying thirty dollars for it. Before we started, William Collins and a Mr. Galt, of Moline, applied to us for passage. They were carpenters, and each had a large tool-chest. Our craft was a large steamboat yawl, but four men and two heavy tool-chests made it draw nearly as much as a steamboat. A number of times we grounded, not being good pilots.

Of our crew of four, two are dead. John Owens died many years ago. William Collins died in Davenport last summer. Mr. Galt still lives in Moline, and has been in feeble health for some years. Neither he nor the writer can last much longer. Fifty years after a man has reached twenty-four does not leave him much vitality.

At eleven o'clock A. M., we pushed off, and set our faces homeward. We took turns at rowing, and, by dusk, saw a nice log cabin on the bank of the river, on the Iowa side, at the head of a slough. We landed and engaged accommodation for the night. Our landlord was a Mr. Cloud, the sheriff of Muscatine County. We were as hungry as wolves, and such a supper! Fried squirrels, hot biscuit, pure white honey, hot coffee, *et cetera*. As we had eaten nothing since morning, we did full justice to the princely meal.

The next morning at daylight, telling our host we would not wait for breakfast, we pulled out for what was then Bloomington, now Muscatine, and soon after sunrise found a little cluster of houses in the woods, one of which was a tavern.[8] Getting our breakfast there, we again pulled out. At about nine o'clock that night, we landed at Oquawka, Illinois, in a cold, driving rain. It was as dark as pitch, and we were met at the landing by about fifty drunken Indians, with firebrands and lanterns, which they waved, yelling and shouting. We thought our scalps in danger; but our dusky escort piloted us to a tavern in safety.

In the morning, the weather was blustering and threatening more rain, but we

[8] The town of Newburg was platted on a portion of the site of Muscatine in 1836. The name was soon changed to Bloomington, but confusion with other postoffices having either the same name or a similar one led the townsmen in 1849 to discard Bloomington for Muscatine.

pushed out once more. The river was rougher than we expected, and, in attempting to cross to the Iowa side, we were nearly swamped. We could make neither shore; but, finding a willow island near by, we hauled our craft up in the willows, and stayed there from sunrise until sunset, when, the wind falling, we started out and went as far as Burlington, where we stayed all night and found good accommodations.

About sunrise, the next day, after a good breakfast, we again put our faces southward. When about a mile below the town, in the middle of the river, I accidentally put my hand into my pocket, and discovered that my pocket-book was missing. On reflection, I remembered putting it under my bolster the night before, and, as it contained all my money, some two hundred and eighty dollars, I told the boys to put me ashore as soon as possible. I made double-quick time for the house, and went directly to the bedroom. The bed had been made, but I soon tore it to pieces. Just then the lady of the house appeared.

"Are you looking for your pocket-book?" she asked. "Here it is; I found it when I made your bed." The woman was honest— no one to blame but myself.

Our next stopping-place was Nauvoo,[9] where we stayed all night. When we started in the morning, the people informed us that our yawl drew too much water to cross the Rapids, and we would likely be wrecked; but we pulled out about sunrise, hoping, some time during the night, to reach Quincy, where we expected to get a steamboat, as we had been told there were two boats running between that place and St. Louis. After working hard all day to reach Quincy, we made a mistake, just before dark, by running into a slough about fifteen miles above the town. After following the slough for a mile, the water failed, and we ran high and dry on a sand-bar, some four hundred feet from the shore. We worked faithfully until midnight, when, tired and discouraged, we concluded to leave the boat there until morning, and waded ashore in water about two feet deep, and, in some places, deeper. We hoped to find a house or cabin, but, after exploring half an hour and yelling until we were hoarse, we ascertained that we were on

[9] Nauvoo was developed and named by the Mormons, fleeing from Missouri, subsequent to the date of this visit. Before the arrival of the Mormons, eastern speculators had planned a town on the site, to which they gave the name of Commerce. It contained only five or six houses, prior to the arrival of the Mormons.

an uninhabited island, so had to pass the night under a big oak tree, with no blankets, wet and hungry, having had nothing to eat since morning. The weather was very cold, it being about the 15th of November. We were a sorry set. We gathered leaves for our bed, limbs and brush to protect us from the sharp wind, and a large pile of stumps and chunks for a fire. We divided ourselves into two watches; one to keep up fires for three hours, while the other slept, and then changed watches.

In the morning, as soon as we could see, we succeeded in getting our craft afloat, and towed her up the river about a mile, where we struck the main stream, and had no further trouble in reaching Quincy. We arrived there about twelve o'clock, noon, nearly starved, having had nothing to eat since sunrise the day before. We ordered our dinner prepared as soon as possible, and were told that the regular dinner would be ready in half an hour. It was a sumptuous dinner, and we did it full justice.

About two o'clock P. M., the steamer *Burlington*, Captain Throckmorton, arrived. The Captain said the boat would return to St. Louis at four P. M. We put our yawl in charge of a warehouse man, to keep until spring. He put it in his warehouse, and during the winter he was burned out, and we lost our boat.

On reaching St. Louis, we found a steamer just ready to start for Cincinnati, and, securing passage, we had no further trouble. I reached home on Saturday morning. On Monday evening, I started East, with my wife and child, to spend the winter in New York and New Jersey, where I was born and spent the days of my childhood. I never spent a happier winter.

In making my trip East, I took a steamer to Wheeling, and thence by stage to Lancaster, Pennsylvania, where I struck the first railroad I ever saw, by which I went to Philadelphia—and such a trip!

There were no separate accommodations for ladies. There were rough bunks for sleeping, which we did not avail ourselves of. Men were drinking, smoking, playing cards, and cursing and swearing. You would have thought you were in a saloon. Such was my first experience in railroad travel, fifty years ago.

Chapter 3

Scarcity of Houses in Davenport in 1839.—Two Small
    Rooms a Mansion.—Outbreak of the Rockingham
    and Missouri Wars.—Marshalling the Davenport
    Patriots.—Revolt Led by the Knight of the Sheet-
    Iron Sword.—Judge Grant and the Horse-Thief.

ABOUT the 1st of March, 1839, I received letters saying the Mississippi
was about to break up, and at once I
commenced making arrangements to return.
Being anxious to add to the population of the
little settlement in Iowa, I persuaded two
brothers-in-law, Wheeler Crane, a carriage-
maker, and Joseph Beach, a painter, also my
two brothers, Lewis and David, stout lads
in those days, to accompany me. Our journey
was without incident until we reached the
Lower Rapids, where we had a tedious time,
getting fast on the rocks, and being nearly a
week getting over.

At last, on the 4th day of April, we reached
our future home, being put ashore on the
bank of the river, about half way between
Perry and Rock Island streets. I remember
the day well. It was a gloomy day, the wind
blew a perfect gale, and everything looked
cheerless.

I found that the man whom I had engaged to put up my house had betrayed me. The money I had left with him to purchase lumber, he had applied to his own use, and there was nothing on the ground but the naked frame which I had purchased in the fall.

The first thing to be done was to find shelter for my wife and child. I succeeded in renting two small rooms, just finished, about twelve feet square, at the corner of Third and Ditch (now Harrison) streets. The rooms were very small and inconvenient for a family of seven persons. We were obliged to go out of doors from one room, to get into the other. They had been built for offices, but in those days we had to do the best we could.

In about two weeks, I had my house weather-boarded and shingled; and, putting down loose boards for a floor, moved in at once, and then finished it, a room at a time. I found the little town a busy place, every one anxious to secure a home. Some settlers, besides myself, came in that spring and a number of houses had been commenced, and the inhabitants of the little town were as active as a swarm of bees.

But the great excitement was the Rockingham War, and, a few weeks later, the Missouri War. I served in both, like a true soldier and patriot. The Rockingham War was tedious, lasting about two years, and four pitched battles were fought, with varying success. The contest was for the county-seat, which Rockingham had and was loth to give up. She had been the emporium of Scott County, outnumbering Davenport in population and business. But two years made a change. Davenport had grown materially, both in population and capital, while poor Rockingham had reached her growth, some of her citizens deserting to the enemy, and, at the last election, sixteen of her people voted for Davenport. As an inducement for the people of Scott County to vote for Davenport, the citizens offered to build the court-house, and present it to the county, free of all expense, promising it should be equal to the court-house across the river, at Stephenson, Illinois; and it was a *fac simile*.

In the early summer we were called upon by the Governor to volunteer to march to the Missouri line, and drive the Missourians from our sacred soil. There was no necessity to repeat the order. We were all fighting men in those days. The war between Rockingham and Davenport was suspended for a short time, and we all united to resist this invasion of our territory by the miserable Missourians. Davenport was selected as headquarters for Scott County. The day appointed for us to meet was a lovely, spring-like morning. Nearly every man in the county was present to be enrolled. Our Colonel, Sam Hedges, made us a patriotic speech; but what a sorry lot of soldiers he had to drill! Not having any guns, many came with pitchforks, scythes, hoes, and clubs. One man had a sheet-iron sword, six or seven feet long. Many were drunk, and all were noisy and disposed to jeer and make fun of our officers. Our Colonel could stand this no longer. All who were drunk, and those improperly armed, were ordered out of the ranks. We who remained were getting hungry, as it was then dinner time, and asked for rations, when we were informed that we would have to furnish our own blankets, whiskey, and hard-tack, which the Government would refund at some future day. This we objected to. We were willing to shed our blood for our beloved Territory, and, if necessary, to kill a few hundred Missourians, but we were not going to do that and board ourselves.

At this juncture, we saw approaching, in solemn column, our fellow-soldiers who had been discharged. They were led by the man with the long sheet-iron sword. They charged on us, and it makes me blush to say, that, notwithstanding we were three to their one, we were badly defeated and scattered in every direction. The Knight of the Sheet-Iron Sword made for our Colonel, and nothing but the Colonel's superior fleetness saved him. As he ran he informed us that we could go home; nothing more would be done until he received further orders.

At this time Congress was in session, and, becoming alarmed at the civil war impending, interfered. The poor barbarians of Missouri, hearing of the hostile demonstrations being made in Davenport and other river towns, withdrew from our Territory. A few months later the Supreme Court met and decided in our favor, and all was peace.[10]

[10] The act of Congress of March 6, 1820, establishing the boundaries of the State of Missouri fixed the northern boundary at the parallel of latitude running "through the rapids of the River Des Moines." The subsequent dispute between the State of Missouri and Iowa Territory turned upon the identification of these rapids, the Iowa contention being that Congress intended the Des Moines Rapids of the Mississippi River, as described by Lieutenant Zebulon Pike in 1805, while the Missourians affirmed that a certain rapid in the Des Moines River itself, some miles farther north was the one intended by Congress. The comic-opera war between the embattled commonwealths soon ended, but the decision of the U. S. Supreme Court awarding the area in dispute to Iowa was not rendered until December, 1848.

Meanwhile, our little village was growing, and the contest between it and Rockingham for the supremacy had been resumed. During February, this year (1839), the first Protestant church was organized—the Presbyterian. During the summer, the Congregationalists and Baptists organized. Neither of these congregations had any church building, but held services in carpenter shops and warehouses. The Catholics had organized in 1838, and erected the first church building in the town.

In May, 1839, hearing that it was court week, and as it was raining hard and I could do no business, I thought I would attend court. There was a small frame building on Ripley Street, at the corner of the alley behind Lahrmann's Hall. It had been built for a carpenter shop, and was used by the Presbyterians for church purposes, and there court was held. I found the little room crowded, and Judge Grant, then "'Squire" Grant, just arranging to defend a horse-thief. The Judge worked cheap in those days. I overheard him whisper to his client: "If you don't give me five dollars before I commence, I won't defend you."

Chapter 4

Brimstone Corner in Davenport.—Some Early Burying-Grounds.—Coffins That Floated.—Establishment of the First Newspaper, the *Iowa Sun.*—A Remarkable Prize Potato, and How It Was Made.—Editor Logan's Righteous Indignation.

NEARLY the whole little settlement, at that time, was about the foot of Ripley Street, which was called Brimstone Corner—I suppose on account of the hot style of preaching indulged in there, in those days.

I found a number of the little band, which I had left there in the fall in perfect health, had gone to that bourne from which no traveler returns. The first ten years I passed in Davenport, there was much more sickness than now. Ten per cent of our population died some years, which was attributed to the breaking up of such large tracts of prairie, producing a miasma which caused fevers, etc.

Our first burying-place was in a corner of a field on the Cook farm, on the north side of the Rockingham Road, nearly opposite the west end of the present Davenport City Cemetery. This was used but a very short time. The next burying-place was at the corner of Sixth and Le Claire streets. It was a miserable selection, and was soon abandoned. I officiated as pall-bearer on two occasions while we buried there. The first was the burial of Judge Mitchell's father. It being early spring, we found the grave half full of water, and had to wait until it was bailed out. But the water came in so fast that the coffin was nearly covered before we could fill the grave. The other was a Dr. Emerson, who died in the Le Claire House, and was the owner of the celebrated slave, Dred Scott.[11]

Our next burial-place was the present Davenport City Cemetery. The writer and a

---

[11] Dr. John Emerson served as assistant surgeon in the U. S. Army from 1833 to Sept. 23, 1842. He purchased Scott at St. Louis in 1833, kept him at Fort Armstrong and at Fort Snelling for several years, and in 1838 returned him to St. Louis. Emerson's sole claim to fame is derived from the posthumous celebrity thrust upon him years after his death by reason of his ownership of the shiftless, happy-go-lucky negro servant, the legal struggle over whose status shook the nation in the fifties. The date of Emerson's death has not been learned, but our author's story implies that it occurred not long after his discharge from the army. His widow subsequently married Charles C. Chaffee, prominent anti-slavery Congressman of Springfield, Mass., to whom this adventitious connection with Scott's ownership proved a matter of much embarrassment.

few other gentlemen, not considering this location desirable (it being too near the rapidly growing city), nor the extent of the grounds sufficient for the purpose, and seeing the need of a city for the dead, combined to secure one that would be a credit to the city when we were dead and gone. It resulted in Oakdale, particulars of which will be given hereafter.[12]

About this time, the first newspaper was established in Davenport. It was called the *Iowa Sun*. Andrew Logan was editor and proprietor. He worked hard to bring the town into notice, with his puffs and marvelous stories of our prolific soil. On my claim was a little piece of ground, some four or five acres, which had been broken up and fenced before I bought. That I immediately planted, and raised the best garden in the county. The two lads, my brothers Lewis and David, seeing the wonderful accounts in the *Iowa Sun* of the productions of other parts of the county, determined to outdo them. We raised, in those days, that king of potatoes, the Neshenocks. It was a large potato, with numerous prongs. Selecting some half-dozen of the largest, the boys fas-

[12] The allusion is to Chapter XLI of the original edition, dealing with the founding of Oakdale Cemetery, which we omit from the present edition.

tened them together with dowels, or wooden pins. When I came home at night, they brought it to me.

"See what we dug to-day!" they said. "Don't that beat anything the *Iowa Sun* has published?"

I replied, "I think it does. What a monster!"

I was completely sold. I said I would take it up in the morning, and give it to Mr. Logan. The next issue of the *Iowa Sun* did full justice to the wonderful production, defying any other soil to produce its equal. The editor said if any one thought it an exaggeration, the skeptic could call and see the monster, as it was hanging up in his office, where he should keep it for a few weeks on exhibition, after which he proposed to try its eating qualities. About two weeks later, during which time the prize potato had been examined by hundreds, our fellow-citizen, John Forrest, Esq., took hold of it, and noticed that one prong was wrong end foremost. So he pulled it apart, and the trick was exposed. Had the boys not made that mistake, the potato would doubtless have been cooked before the joke was discovered. It created a vast amount of fun, and a big laugh at the expense of the *Iowa Sun*.

It is said that Mr. Logan abstained from eating potatoes for over a month.

After the discovery, Mr. Forrest hastened up town to my store. He said: "Burrows, they have a big joke on you, down town, about that big potato." He then told me what had occurred. I told him I was sold with the rest, for I knew nothing about it. He advised me to keep away from Logan for a few days, or I would lose my scalp.

Chapter 5

The Interesting History of the Rev. Michael Hummer.
—His Eccentric Habits and High Temper.—How He
Fell Out with the Iowa Citizens Over a Church Bell.
—The Pleasing Ballad of Hummer's Bell.

IN looking over the *Annals of Iowa*, to
refresh my memory, I saw an article on
the Rev. Michael Hummer, who was a
very early settler, and, I believe, taught a
private school or academy in Stephenson,
now Rock Island City, Illinois, in 1838. In
the spring of 1839, he received a call from the
Presbyterian Church in Davenport, just organized, to preach for them for six months,
which he accepted. He was a very talented
man, and was considered, for years, the
ablest clergyman in the State; but he was
very peculiar. He possessed a high temper,
and did not hesitate to show it if occasion
required.

After fulfilling his appointment with the
Presbyterian Church of Davenport, the Rev.
Mr. Hummer accepted a call to the Presbyterian Church in Iowa City. While occupying that position, he was sent East to solicit
aid for a church they were about to erect.
Among other donations, he procured a

church-bell, which was brought out and properly hung in the church-steeple. After some time, he and the congregation falling out, in his imperious style he claimed possession of the bell as his property, which claim the Church contested. The Rev. Mr. Hummer left Iowa City, and went to Keokuk. After a good deal of wrangling, he appeared in Iowa City, one day, with a wagon and ladder, and, going to the Church, with the aid of his ladder he succeeded in getting into the steeple, and, unfastening the bell, lowered it into the wagon. The citizens immediately took the ladder down, and drove his team away with the bell, which they hid in the Iowa River, leaving the Rev. Mr. Hummer to his meditations, in the steeple. So many persons have inquired of me about this affair, that I thought it would be interesting to weave the facts into this narrative. I copy from the *Annals of Iowa*:

The future historian of Johnson County will, doubtless, devote at least one chapter to that talented but most unscrupulous individual, yclept the Rev. Michael Hummer, with whom, in the minds of the oldest inhabitants of Iowa City, his bell is so inseparably connected.

That bell, famed both in caricature and story, as the highly prized jewel of Hummer, so singularly abducted, and so secretly and securely concealed, was the subject of some hastily written versicles, entitled "Hummer's

Bell," that, at the time, attained considerable popularity, not so much, perhaps, from any intrinsic merit of their own, as from the incident that gave rise to them.

The first copy of the brochure was given by me to Stephen Whicher, Esq., who, upon his own volition, had a number privately printed and circulated, in which, greatly to my annoyance, several changes and interpolations appeared, totally at variance with the original; and, as it is extremely doubtful whether a correct and perfect copy can, at this time, be found, I have thought it might be sufficiently interesting, as one of the reminiscences of former years, to have "Hummer's Bell," like the fly preserved in amber, embalmed in the pages of the *Annals of Iowa.*

A part of the first verse was the improvisation of the Hon. John P. Cook, the legal vocalist of the day, who, upon hearing a ludicrous story of the bell's departure, broke out in song, to the infinite merriment of the members of the bar present, and, in his sonorous and mellifluent tones, sang the first six lines, to the well-known popular air of Moore's "Evening Bells." Stephen Whicher, Esq., who made one of the merry company, carefully noted down the fragmentary carol, and, meeting me soon afterwards, earnestly solicited me to complete the song, as he termed it. His request was immediately complied with, and in a few moments, the whole versified story of the bell was told in an impromptu production, of which I append a copy, *verbatim et literatum,* from the original MS. now lying before me, and which has never been out of my possession:

HUMMER'S BELL

Ah, Hummer's bell! Ah, Hummer's bell!
How many a tale of woe 'twould tell
Of Hummer driving up to town,
To take the brazen jewel down.

133

And when high up in his belfre-e,
They moved the ladder, yes, sir-e-e;
Thus, while he towered aloft, they say
The bell took wings and flew away.

Ah, Hummer's bell! Ah, Hummer's bell!
The bard thy history shall tell;
How at the East, by Hummer's sleight,
Donation, gift, and widow's mite,
Made up the sum that purchased *thee*,
And placed *him* in the ministry.
But funds grew low, while dander riz;
Thy clapper stopped, and so did his.

Ah, Hummer's bell! Ah, Hummer's bell!
We've heard thy last, thy funeral knell;
And what an aching void is left—
Of bell and Hummer both bereft.
Thou, deeply sunk in running stream,
Him in a Swedenborgian dream.
Both are submerged—both, to our cost,
Alike to sense and reason lost.

Ah, Hummer's bell! Ah, Hummer's bell!
Hidden unwisely, but too well;
Alas, tou'rt gone! Thy silvery tone
No more responds to Hummer's groan.
But yet remains one source of hope,
For Hummer left a fine bell-rope,
Which may be used, if such our luck,
To noose our friend at Keokuk.

W. H. T.

    I was well acquainted with Mr. Hummer
when he lived in Davenport, and always had
a great deal of charity for him, as I always

thought him *non compos mentis*. When he left Iowa City, he moved to Keokuk, and, after creating a great deal of excitement in propagating his views on spiritualism, which he embraced in his latter days, he became so unpopular that he went to Missouri, not far from Kansas City, since which time I have lost track of him, but have been told he is dead. The celebrated bell, I understand, has been recovered from the sands of the Iowa River, and is now in possession of the Mormons, at Salt Lake.

Chapter 6

Breaking a Scott County Claim.—The First Davenport Vegetable Wagon.—Engaging in the Mercantile Business.—Testing a Rockingham Doctor.—Sociability of the Old Settlers.—The Delights of the Early Straw Ride.

MY two brothers-in-law returned East in a few months. They were not made of pioneer timber, and said this country was only fit for Indians. On the 1st day of January, 1840, the population was about five hundred, with one hundred houses. During the year 1839, I devoted my time to breaking and improving my claim. Soon after my arrival, in the spring, I went over to Henderson Grove, Illinois, and purchased two cows, and two yoke of oxen to plow my land; also, a lot of poultry. On my return, I could find no feed in the place, so took a trip to New Boston, Illinois, and laid in a supply of corn, etc. By this time my money was about exhausted, and, having my five-acre tract well planted with garden-truck, much more than my family could use, I concluded to start a vegetable-wagon, and sent my youngest brother, David A. Burrows, then a lad of about twelve years, up town, every

136

morning, with a load of vegetables, which he took from house to house. This was well patronized, and proved a relief to the community, as the great cry in those early days was for something to eat. So D. A. Burrows has the credit of being the first vegetable peddler of Davenport.

I had expected, when I came here, to turn my attention to farming, but found my wife too delicate for that mode of life, so concluded to go into some kind of mercantile business, in the spring. During the fall and winter I cut down some oak trees on my place, and hewed out a frame for the building I occupied for so many years, on Front Street. I then hired a carpenter, a Mr. Rumbold, and worked with him, and by the opening of navigation it was ready for occupancy. Early in March I started for Cincinnati, to see if I could not get some supplies for a store. I had no money. My little all was invested. I had a cousin, John A. D. Burrows, of Burrows & Hall, Pearl Street, Cincinnati. They were the largest wholesale grocers of Cincinnati. He said: "Take all you want out of our stock." So I laid in a full supply of groceries.

I also found a man who had received, in a trade, an old stock of boots and shoes, which had been well culled over. He wanted to sell to me, and would sell cheap, but I refused to purchase such an outlandish stock of goods. If he wished, however, I told him, I would take them on commission, and sell them on halves, which I did. I do not think he could have sold them in Cincinnati in one hundred years.

During the summer of 1839, while the Rockingham feud was most intense, my wife was taken dangerously ill, from the fatigue and exposure to which she had been subjected. Davenport had two physicians, but neither of them seemed to do her any good; and as Dr. Barrows, then of Rockingham, was considered the ablest physician in the Territory, I determined to call him, Rockingham or no Rockingham, which was a very unpopular thing to do. I was warned that it was unsafe to employ him—I would have to watch him, as he would pocket everything he could lay his hands on. He was given about as good a character as Ben Butler received in New Orleans during the late war.

The good doctor responded promptly. My wife improved rapidly under his treatment, and from then until Dr. Fountain married my daughter, he was our family physician. The doctor was then in the prime of life, and stood at the head of his profession.

In the early days of this county, the old settlers were a much more social and liberal community than the population of the present day. The pioneer was kind-hearted and generous, ever ready to assist and help. The needy settler always found an open hand and a kind heart in his neighbor, and if there was sickness in the family, or a cabin to be built, there were plenty of willing hands to assist.

The pioneer settlers acted on the principle that all work and no play makes Jack a dull boy, and they had their seasons of fun and enjoyment; especially was that the case in our long, dull winters. Sleighing parties, hunting parties, balls, and visiting one another, were frequent events; and the writer, while generally having as much business as he could attend to, will have to admit that he repeatedly neglected his business, in those days, and, filling his bob-sled full of clean straw, packed his wife and about a dozen other ladies in, like sardines, until the sled was filled, they sitting on the straw, and would then drive twenty or twenty-five miles, to spend the day with some pioneer friends, leaving early in the morning and returning at midnight—a jolly crowd.

Farmers living on the Wapsie and at the Groves used to visit the city every week or two, generally on Saturday, and spend the day in trading, and, many of them, in drinking. Some of the stores, for the sake of drawing trade, kept barrels of whisky in their warehouses, each barrel with a tin cup under it, where any one could help himself, free. There was no beer in those days, or there would have been less drunkenness.[13] Burrows & Prettyman never sold a drop of liquor during their business career, and some farmers would not trade with us for that reason, and we informed them we did not care for their patronage. We had all the business we wanted.

[13] Prior to the Civil War beer-drinking in the United States was confined to the German element of the population, whose social habits were regarded with disdain by native Americans. During the war, Congress levied very severe duties on distilled liquors and much more moderate ones on beer and ale. At the same time the German-Americans co-operated loyally in the conduct of the war, with the result that much of the earlier prejudice against them moderated or disappeared. The two influences of financial advantage and gratitude for patriotic service, combined with the perception that beer was less harmful to the consumer than whisky, to which America had chiefly been addicted hitherto, brought about the general use of beer as a beverage in America. See Frederick Merk, *Economic History of Wisconsin During the Civil War Decade* (Madison, 1916), 152–55.

Chapter 7

Struggles in the Mercantile Trade.—The First Store, and How It Was Stocked.—Another Trip to Cincinnati.—Rudimentary Banking in Davenport.—Trade Begins to Pick Up.

MY little store, in the meantime, was taking root, and, in October, it was necessary for me to return to Cincinnati, to lay in my winter stock. I had succeeded much better than either myself or friends expected, and I went to Cincinnati able to pay my friends who had kindly trusted me. I had no trouble in getting all the goods I wanted. My good cousin, John A. D. Burrows, has been dead many years, but I always looked upon him as my earliest benefactor. He was a noble, generous man—a man of means and large heart. His father was wealthy, and he himself was the head of the largest wholesale grocery in the city. He always seemed to take an interest in me.

After selecting what I wanted in his line, he said, "John, do you think you could manage a stock of dry goods?" I said I thought I could, so he took me in next door, to the establishment of A. W. Sprague & Co., the largest wholesale dry goods house in the city, a branch of the great manufacturing firm of A. W. Sprague & Co., of Rhode Island. He said:

"This is my cousin, J. M. D. Burrows, of Wisconsin Territory. He is just commencing business, and I want you to sell him a stock of dry goods. It is not likely that he can meet his notes promptly, but I will be responsible for all you sell him."

They said "All right!" and we made an appointment for the next morning, at ten o'clock. Turning to me, he said:

"I shall select the goods, myself. You remember I was in the dry goods business once, and, besides, I do not like to trust you to their tender mercies."

At the appointed hour we went in, and he selected a stock of dry goods for me, second to none in Davenport.

Another great help to me, at this time, was the assistance I received from James Glaspell, Sr., the progenitor of the Glaspell family. He was an excellent man; one of the salt of the earth—a man in whom there was no guile. He lived under the bluff, a half-mile below me. He called on me the day before I left home, and said: "Neighbor Burrows, I want you to do me a favor. You are going to Cincinnati. When I left Covington, Kentucky, I made an auction of my cattle, farming implements, etc. They were sold on a year's credit, and my agent writes to me that he has made some collections. Now, will you be so good as to cross over to Covington, and get what money he has on hand? I shall not need it for some time, and if it is any help to you, you can use it."

I collected about a thousand dollars, and used it in getting many articles I needed, outside the regular line. I returned with the largest and best selected stock of goods in Davenport.

When I reported to my neighbor, Glaspell, he seemed much pleased at the result, and said he probably would not need his money for a year, and when he did, he would give me a month's notice. He would not receive any interest, considering that I was doing him a favor, as he was afraid to keep so much money in the house. During the year, having a large family, he took a good deal of it out in goods from the store.

At this time, and for a number of years afterward, we had no bank. Some of our farmers had money that they were afraid to keep at their homes. Especially was this the case at the Groves, and on the Wapsie, and even in Clinton County. The farmers, consequently, brought their money in and deposited it with me, the same as if I were a

143

banker. This, when I was just starting and my means were limited, was a great help to my business.

During the winter I did a good business. Having become acquainted in Clinton and Jackson counties, I began to draw trade from there.

Chapter 8

Servant Girls Almost as Hard to Get in the Forties as They Are Now.—A Specimen Hunt for Help When It Was Needed Badly.—Help, When Found, Was Better Then Than Now, Though.

I WILL mention one little incident that occurred in 1840, showing the difficulties and hardships of those very early days. Female hired help was not to be obtained. I assisted my wife all I could—probably did as much house-work as she did. She was not strong, and was unaccustomed to such work. In July, my son, Elisha, was born. We had no help, but had been looking for a girl for months. Mrs. John Owens and Mrs. Ebenezer Cook, one living a mile above and the other a mile below our house, took turns in taking care of my wife and the child, one during the daytime, and the other at night; but they had to neglect their own families to do so. I knew this state of things could not last, and determined to find help at any cost. Having no clerk yet in my store, I was obliged to lock it up and, with the key in my pocket, rode three days all over the county in search of a girl.

The first day, I went up to Le Claire, canvassing Pleasant Valley thoroughly, but with no success. The next day I rode through the southern part of the county and Blue Grass, as far as there was any settlement, but all in vain. On this trip, I was told there was a family in Walnut Grove, where there were two grown daughters, who, it was understood, sometimes went to nurse sick neighbors. I determined to go there, and, on leaving home the third day, told the ladies that if I did not get back that night they need not be alarmed, as I would not return without help.

When I reached Walnut Grove, at about half-past eleven in the morning, I found the coziest and neatest farm-house I had yet seen in the Territory, and Mrs. Heller, with two full-grown, healthy looking daughters, all as neat as wax. The house was better furnished than any I had seen. The window curtains and bed-spread were as white as the driven snow. The floors shone like silver. I introduced myself, and made known my business. I told Mrs. Heller my situation was desperate—that I had come for one of her daughters, and would not go away without one. She said she would leave the matter altogether with their father, who was at work in the field, half a mile away. She invited me to sit down and wait until he came in to dinner, which would be in about half an hour. But I said:

"My business is too important to admit of delay. I will go to the field."

I found Mr. Heller cradling wheat, and not a stranger, as I supposed, for when we met we recognized each other, having been on a jury together, a few months before. I told my story in as few words as possible.

He hung his cradle on the fence, and we went to the house, as it was about dinner-time. He said he would like to help me out of my trouble; that they were working hard to open a farm, and he was not able to do much for his daughters, and whatever they earned they had to clothe themselves with; but they never had gone away from home except to help sick neighbors sometimes. He knew from what he had seen of me that I would treat them well, and he would be glad to have one of them go with me to relieve me. When we arrived at the house he told his daughters what I wanted, and that it would please him if one of them would go with me. The youngest one spoke up and said, "I will go;" and I was happy. She returned with me, and lived in my family seven years, until she married. My wife and myself always looked upon her as a sister or a child. She married one of the most respectable men of the day, an owner of a good farm and a member of the State Legislature. They are both living in Davenport at the present time. That young woman is now nearly seventy years old.

Chapter 9

Beginning of the Produce Trade in Davenport.—Buying Wheat and Hogs on a Venture.—Success Despite the Discouraging Predictions of Friends.—I Hire R. M. Prettyman.

IN the winter of 1840, I did as good a business as any one in the town. During the winter, our farmers were compelled to sell a little wheat and some pork, to obtain money to buy medicine, pay postage, etc.; so that year, Horace Bradley, of Pleasant Valley, still living, brought to Davenport the first load of wheat that was ever sold in the town for commercial purposes. A few others were compelled to sell some dressed hogs. I bought that wheat, and I bought those hogs; and this was the commencement of the produce trade of Davenport.

At that time, there were only some three or four stores in the little village. My brother merchants laughed at me. Some said I was a fool—"What is he going to do with the produce?" Well, to tell the truth, I hardly knew, myself; but one thing I did know, and one thing I felt, that this country had to be settled up, and to accomplish this, some one must buy the farmers' surplus, or

it would remain a wilderness. So I made up
my mind I would devote myself to this purpose, and I bought, that fall, all the surplus
wheat and pork and other produce offered.

The wheat I hauled to the Rockingham
Mill, and had it manufactured into flour,
which, with my pork, white beans, etc., I
took to Prairie du Chien, and sold to the Fur
Company and the Indians. The Fur Company was controlled by a Mr. Dousman,[14]
whom I found to be a gentleman, and for a
number of years he purchased produce of
me every trip. I also sold poultry to the
officers at Fort Crawford. My wife having
raised, one year, seventy-five more turkeys
than we needed, I took them to the Fort, and
sold them for a dollar apiece.

In the spring of 1841, D. C. Eldridge, who
kept a hotel called the White Hall, on Main
Street, on the very ground now occupied by
the *Democrat* newspaper building, introduced
R. M. Prettyman to me as a very capable
and worthy young man, seeking employment; that he had been with him some time,
but did not like his occupation; he preferred
a situation in a business house. I had never

[14] Hercules L. Dousman, agent of the American Fur
Company at Prairie du Chien, and long a leading
merchant and citizen. He died, Sept. 12, 1868. His
fine residence at Prairie du Chien is still preserved.

seen him before. I told Mr. Prettyman that
I had not intended employing any one at
that time; that my business would not justify such an expense. It was growing rapidly, and I would soon be compelled to have
some help. He said he would like to come
with me, and I need not pay him anything
until my business would justify it. I told
him I would think of the matter, and that he
might call the next morning.

I was then living on my claim, a mile from
the store, but always had my store open
about daylight—the first in town. I carried
my dinner in a little tin pail, and did not
get home until dark. I knew I needed him,
but I was economizing, struggling to get
a foot-hold, and did not want to hire any
one to do what I could do myself; yet I
wisely concluded to engage him. He commenced at once, and I soon saw I had taken
a wise step.

That summer I visited the trading-posts
above, a number of times. Fort Snelling,[15]
Prairie du Chien, and Snake Hollow, in the
lead regions, were my principal points. At

[15] Fort Snelling at the junction of the Minnesota and
Mississippi rivers, near St. Paul, was established in
1819, being originally called Fort St. Anthony. It still
remains an important military station of the U. S.
Army.

that time Snake Hollow[16] was about the best point I found in which to sell produce. Besides selling to the traders, I traded bacon, flour, beans, etc., with the Indians for feathers and beeswax, which I sold in Cincinnati. I could now leave home on these expeditions, feeling all was right there, for a more honest, capable, and devoted man than R. M. Prettyman, no man ever had in his employ. If he had owned the concern, he could not have been more devoted to its interests. At the end of the first month, I told him to credit himself with forty dollars as his first month's wages, which at that time was liberal compensation.

The seed planted by the pioneers soon took root and began to spread. The produce business enlarged itself rapidly, and my great trouble was to know where to place the products. There was no Chicago[17] then, not

---

[16] Present-day Potosi, Wis., about fifteen miles upriver from Dubuque. During the second quarter of the nineteenth century it was one of the leading lead-mining centers of southwestern Wisconsin, and was variously known as Snake Hollow, Snake Diggings, and Potosi.

[17] The growth of modern Chicago began in 1833. A wild boom of several years' duration was followed by a like wild depression, in whose depths the City was at this time (1840) wallowing. The first section (to the Des Plaines River) of Chicago's first railroad, the

much of a market in St. Louis, and I had to make frequent trips to every landing north of Davenport as far as Fort Snelling. St. Paul at that time contained only a wood-yard and one log cabin, where the Indians got their whisky and tobacco.[18]

Galena and Chicago Union, was opened in 1848, and the canal connecting Lake Michigan with the Illinois River the same year. Although there was, in fact, a Chicago in 1840, but few highways between it and the Mississippi existed to make trading relations possible.

[18] Pierre Parrant bought a hovel on the site of St. Paul in June, 1838, and two years later a settlement of French-Canadians was made on the site. In 1841 Father Galtier built a log chapel, dedicated to St. Paul, and from it the future city acquired its name. As late as 1845 the settlement contained but 30 families, almost all of them French. Parrant was familiarly known as Pig's Eye, and the settlement which grew up around his cabin was known by the same name.

Chapter 10

A Trip North in 1841.—Trading with the Fur Company.
—A Perilous Journey Home, with Pocketsful of
Gold.—Nearly Drowned in a Canoe.—The Suspected
Farmer, and the Power of Prayer.—A Stranger in
the Dark.—Home at Last.

IN the spring of 1841, I found my means
all locked up in produce—corn, flour,
pork, bacon, etc.,—and that it would be
necessary for me to realize on a good portion
of my stock early, in order to replenish my
store. The spring was late that year, and it
was well along in April before I could get a
boat. At last I found the steamer *Smelter*,
Captain Scribe Harris. The Captain said he
was going up as far as Prairie du Chien, and
I concluded to go with him. On our way up,
we went into Snake Hollow, where I made a
profitable sale. On my arrival at Prairie du
Chien, I found the Fur Company had received no spring supplies, and was in need of
provisions. During the forenoon I sold them
my entire stock, all at fair prices, and received my pay, cash down, in gold and silver.
Captain Harris, finding the Wisconsin
River very high, decided to go up that
stream, being offered a big lot of shot from a

shot-tower up that river.[19] He told me he might be gone a week. I was now in a quandary how to get home. There was no boat above, and none expected from below. On inquiry, I learned that at some Grove, about twelve miles from there, a stage would pass through at three o'clock next day. I made up my mind that I would take that stage.

After breakfast, I procured some strong brown paper, went to my room and wrapped each piece of money separately, and then made them into small rolls, and loaded each pocket with all it would hold, and tied the rest in a strong handkerchief. I went back to the Fur Company's office and got them to exchange the silver for gold as far as they could.

The great part of the Company funds paid out in those days was Spanish dollars. I was anxious to get my gold and silver home, as it was ten per cent premium, our paper currency being nothing but Wildcat issued at Green Bay.[20]

[19] The first shot-tower in the West, if not in America, was built at Herculaneum, Mo., in 1809. In 1831 Daniel Whitney, an enterprising merchant and promoter of Green Bay, in company with other associates, established a shot-tower at Helena, Wisconsin, which flourished for many years. For its history see *Wis. Hist. Colls.*, XIII, 335–74.

[20] The Spanish dollar, first coined in 1728, circulated throughout the commercial world and was widely

At eleven o'clock A.M., I took a lunch and started, going three miles down the river, where I struck the Wisconsin ferry. The river was booming high, and seemed to run with the velocity of a locomotive. I could find no ferryman. I rang the bell, off and on, for half an hour. The ferryman's canoe was there, with a good pair of paddles, and I saw that I would either have to go back or paddle myself over, so I launched that canoe and shoved off.

I was never in a canoe before, and did not know how to handle it, but soon found that I had to sit very still, flat in the bottom, in the water, as it leaked. The canoe kept going round and round, and every few minutes would dip some water. Meanwhile the current was conveying me swiftly down to the Mississippi.

accepted as a recognized medium of exchange. The American silver dollar is its direct descendant. The author's statement indicates that as recently as the middle of the nineteenth century it was in common use throughout the Mississippi Valley.

Wildcat currency was painfully familiar to our grandfathers. It consisted of banknotes which were commonly issued at some obscure place, or at least were circulated at some point distant from the place of issue, in order to deter the holders of the notes from presenting them for redemption. Frequently they had no actual cash security back of them. Certain of their characteristics are set forth in the further course of the author's narrative.

I thought I was lost. I would have given all my money to be safe on either shore, and why I was not drowned was always a mystery to me; but I suppose my time had not come.

I noticed that as the canoe whirled around, each time brought me nearer to the shore. I also began to manage the paddles to better advantage, and soon struck the willows, which I caught, and pulled the canoe as near the shore as I could; then jumped overboard, and got on dry land as soon as possible. After I had straightened up and let the water drain from my clothing, I set forward for the stage again. About a mile farther on, I came to a small creek or stream. There was no bridge, and it could not be forded, as the banks were straight up and down. The water was fully four or five feet deep. After examining up and down the stream, I saw there was no way but to jump it. I chose the narrowest place I could find, pitched my bundle of money across, and then took a run and jumped! Just made it, and that was all.

As I struck the edge of the bank, one of my coat-pockets gave way, and fell, with its heavy contents, in four feet of water. I hunted up a forked stick, and, luckily, the lining having gone with the pocket, soon fished it out, and made for the stage-house, which I reached without further trouble, only to find that the stage had gone!

I then determined to make my way to Dubuque on foot, where I hoped to get a boat. About dark, I saw a cabin just ahead, where I decided to stay all night. I was puzzled what to do with my money, as I feared I would be robbed—perhaps murdered. My first thought was to hide it in a pile of brush I saw near, but I was afraid some one would see me, so resolved to share its fate.

On applying to the woman at the cabin for lodging, she referred me to her husband, who was at the barn. I interviewed him. He said I could stay. He was a rough-looking man, and I did not feel very safe.

After he had taken care of the stock, we went to the house together. Supper was nearly ready. I took a seat by the fire, with my bundle by my side. In a few minutes supper was announced, and I sat down at the table, carrying my bundle with me.

Just then, two as hard-looking men as I ever saw came in and sat down at the table, eyeing me sharply. I was becoming a little alarmed, when the proprietor asked a blessing on the meal, and no human being can realize what a relief came to my mind. All anxiety about my money or my life passed away.

Early next morning, at break of day, I was on the road again, determined to reach Dubuque some time that night. At noon it began to rain, but I persevered. At sundown I reached Parsons' Ferry, fifteen miles above Dubuque. Being on the Wisconsin side, it was necessary to cross there, and again I was troubled to arouse the ferryman. After nearly an hour, he answered my signal, and set me over. By this time it was pitch dark, and raining hard, and I had fifteen miles yet to make. I took the middle of the road. The mud was very deep, and the darkness so great a man could not be seen six inches from you. While plodding along, with my bundle in one hand and a big club, which I used as a cane, in the other, I ran against a man. Neither of us saw the other. I never was a coward, but was never more startled in my life. My heart choked me so that I could not articulate plainly; but, with my club raised, I stammered out, "What do you want?"

I saw, from his mumbling and incoherent reply, that he was drunk, and I walked around him and pushed on my way.

At eleven o'clock at night I reached Dubuque, having walked seventy-five miles in thirty-six hours. I was not acquainted in Dubuque, and did not know where to find a hotel. After wandering about some time, I met a man whom I asked to direct me to the best tavern in the place. He did so, but as I did not know the names of the streets or the location, I could not find the house. I had become tired and bewildered, when I met another man. I said to him:

"My friend, I wish to find the best hotel in town. I am a stranger, and have been hunting your town over for some time, up one street and down another, until I have become confused. Will you be kind enough to go with me and show me?"

He cheerfully did so. It was a first-rate house; the best I had yet seen above St. Louis. I had a nice, clean room, all to myself, and the table was well provided for. I told the landlord he need not go to any trouble to cook anything for me; that although I had had nothing to eat since daylight, I would be satisfied with a cold lunch and a cup of hot coffee. On going to bed, I gave orders not to be called in the morning, unless there was a boat going down.

I did not waken until noon the next day, when my landlord knocked at the door and said there was a boat at the landing, going down. I was so sore and stiff I could scarcely dress myself, and could only get down stairs by sliding down the banister. I found the boat would not leave until three o'clock, so told my kind landlord I would take dinner with him, instead of eating on the boat.

We started toward night, and reached home the next forenoon. I was so lame and crippled for ten days that I had as much as I could do to attend to my business.

Such were the trials and labors of a pioneer merchant of those early days.

Chapter 11

Hard Times and Over-Production.—Bidding for the
Government Contracts for Forts Snelling and Craw-
ford.—Timely Aid from Antoine Le Claire and
Colonel Davenport.—The Atchison Brothers and
Their Methods.

THE times were very hard then, and for
some years after. Our land had just been
brought into market by the Government, and all the money in the country went
into the land office. Some of our best farmers
paid fifty per cent for money to enter their
lands, and were kept poor for years paying
interest. Meanwhile, they used all the money
they could get hold of, to break, fence, and
stock their farms, spending as little as they
could with the merchant, and what trading
they did was generally on a year's credit.

No one can realize the difficulties of doing
a produce business in those days. We had
no railroads. Everything had to be moved
by water, and, of course, had to be held all
winter. To keep up with the rapid growth of
the country and provide for the surplus, required not only money and credit, but, what
in those days was more important than
either, nerve.

In the year 1841, I saw the amount of wheat and pork was going to be double as much as ever before, and I was very solicitous as to what I should do with it. I saw in the St. Louis *Republican* that the Government invited proposals for furnishing Fort Snelling and Fort Crawford with a year's supply of pork, flour, beans, soap, vinegar, candles, and numerous other articles. I considered the matter, and could think of no reason why Scott County could not furnish the pork, flour, beans, etc., as well as St. Louis, which had furnished them heretofore. So I decided to put in a bid, if I could find any one to go on my bonds, which were heavy. I interviewed Mr. Le Claire[21] and Colonel Davenport, and told them what I was thinking of. If I could accomplish it, and get a contract and fill it from home pro-

[21] Antoine Le Claire was born at St. Joseph (near modern Niles), Michigan, the son of a French father and a Potawatomi mother. He supported the American cause in the War of 1812 and during it, or soon afterward, entered the service of the U. S. Indian Department. He served as interpreter on many occasions, speaking numerous Indian languages in addition to French and English. The grant of Indian reservations on the site of Davenport and elsewhere eventually rendered him wealthy, and for many years he was one of Davenport's most public-spirited citizens. He died there, Sept. 25, 1868.

duction, it would be a grand thing for both the town and the county, and be the means of circulating a good deal of money, of which the people at that time were sadly in need. Those gentlemen, always ready and anxious to do anything that would settle up and advance the prosperity of the country, were much pleased with my suggestion, and said they would stand by me.

I put in bids for both forts, referring, as to my responsibility, to Colonel Davenport and Antoine Le Claire. As I was going to Cincinnati, I wrote to them that if my bids were accepted to address me there, as I wished to purchase in that market such supplies as could not be procured at home. On my arrival, I found a communication from the Department at Washington, saying my bid for Fort Snelling had been accepted. On my return home, I found that John Atchison, who had been the successful contractor of both forts for two or three years previous, had been in town three days awaiting my return. I got home about dark. My wife told me that Ebenezer Cook had left word that I had better avoid meeting Atchison until I had seen Cook; so after supper I walked down to Mr. Cook's house, about a mile on the Rockingham Road. He informed me that Atchison was very anxious to buy me out. He did not care about furnishing the supplies so much as he did for the transportation. The Atchison Brothers owned the largest and most magnificent steamboat on the Upper Mississippi, called the *Amaranth*. They had been very successful in controlling both the Government's and the Fur Company's freight, and my success was a great surprise to them. In the morning, Atchison made his appearance. I refused to sell, telling him my only object in taking the contract was to make an outlet for my winter accumulation. After talking the matter over all day, I sold out on these conditions: He to pay me a bonus of twenty-five hundred dollars, cash down; I to furnish the flour, pork, and beans, for which he was to pay me contract price, less the transportation, and pay me cash down on delivery to his boat, the next June, the time specified by the Government.

I now went to work hauling my wheat to Rockingham Mill, and scouring the country for hogs. My cooperage—pork, flour, and bean barrels—I had all manufactured at home, giving employment to a number of coopers. This, with the money I had received from Atchison and scattered among the farmers for hogs, wheat, beans, etc., gave our little village and the county a decided boom.

Chapter 12

Orders Made and Countermanded by the Government.
—The Difficulty of Finding Hogs for Market.—
Another Deal with Atchison Brothers.—Dark Days
for the Farmers.—Success in the End.

THE Government, in making contracts, reserved the privilege of increasing or diminishing any article one-third, by giving sixty days' notice. When I sold out to Atchison, in the fall, I wrote to the Department at Washington what I had done; that the Atchison Brothers had been contractors for a number of years previous, and that the contract was in good hands. The Department replied that it had nothing to do with the Atchisons; that it was a matter between them and myself, the Government looking to me for the fulfillment of my contract.

In January, I received notice from Washington that the pork would be increased one-third. I immediately notified the Atchisons, and asked them if they wished me to furnish it, and on the same terms as the other. They replied that they did. I then went to work to canvass the whole county. The hog crop was about over. I rummaged Clinton, Jackson, Cedar, and Linn counties, in Iowa, and Rock

Island County, Illinois; also buying any pork I could find in the hands of the packers in Rockingham, and of John Seaman in Davenport.

I succeeded in my efforts, and had the whole ready for delivery, when I received notice from the proper authorities that my pork contract was reduced one-third, to its original quantity. I received notice from the Atchisons, on the 1st of June, to be ready with my stuff, as the *Amaranth* would be along in a few days. She arrived according to appointment.

Ebenezer Cook, at that time, was my attorney and friend. He seemed much pleased with my success in this contract. He had drawn up all my papers, both my proposals to the Government, and all others. He was a long-headed, shrewd man, and cautious in all his transactions.

He said to me: "I have ascertained that the Atchisons are somewhat shaky. Don't you deliver until you are paid."

When the boat landed, I pointed out the freight, and asked to be excused for a few minutes, and hurrying back to the store, I gave Prettyman the items and prices; told him to make out a bill as soon as possible, which was quickly done; and I took the bill, together with the agreement they had made

167

with me, specifying they were to pay on delivery, and hurried to the boat. The Atchisons were just preparing to load. I presented my bill. Atchison said: "Well, I did not expect to pay until we returned."

I told him that would not suit me. My spring payments were past due. I had depended upon his paying me, according to his agreement, and I could not get along without it. After waiting nearly half a day, he said he had some money on the boat that he had promised some one in Galena. He would give me that, as far as it went, and a draft on St. Louis for the balance. I said if the St. Louis house was satisfactory, I would accept his proposition. The paper was all right—drawn on a first-class steamboat house, and was promptly paid.

We loaded up that afternoon, and steamed up the river with the provisions for both forts. I went up to Fort Snelling, and saw that my contract was filled to the letter. This operation, together with the little capital I had succeeded in accumulating before, set me on my feet, and I was now able to walk instead of crawl. Besides the twenty-five hundred dollars bonus, I got one-third more for my pork than I could have got in the open market, as there was a heavy decline in provisions in the spring of that year.

During the summer, good, sound, sweet, smoked shoulders would not net more than one cent a pound, and our steamboats bought more or less for fuel, saying they were cheaper than wood. Those were hard times for both the farmer and the merchant: wheat selling from thirty to forty cents a bushel; dressed hogs, one dollar to one dollar and fifty cents per hundred pounds; nice dressed quails plenty at twenty-five cents a dozen; dressed prairie-chickens at five cents each; good fresh butter at five to eight cents a pound; eggs, from three to five cents a dozen; and many farmers paying fifty per cent for money which they had borrowed to enter their land. Those were dark days in Iowa, and there was no let-up for a number of years.

Besides what I had made on my pork, I made a reasonable profit on the flour and beans, and I was happy. I always considered this as the best and most successful operation I ever undertook, and it benefited Scott County as much as it did me, as the money I obtained was scattered all over the county paying for produce. A little money at that time went a great way and accomplished much good.

Chapter 13

My Introduction to Daniel T. Newcomb.—A Hurried Night Ride to Muscatine.—Mr. Newcomb's Hospitality and Enterprise.—Some Early Real Estate Transactions in Davenport.—The Newcomb Memorial Chapel.—Mrs. Newcomb.

IN the spring of 1842, I had occasion to make a very sudden and unexpected visit to Muscatine. I left Davenport after dark with a horse and buggy, and it was necessary I should reach Muscatine by sunrise in the morning, to meet a certain steamboat. The night was fearfully dark, the road bad and full of stumps, and I made slow headway. About midnight, when half way, I ran over a stump and was upset. I then concluded I would have to stop at the first house until daylight. I had never been over the road before, but seeing a log cabin on the bank of the river, near by, I began pounding at the door. Presently I heard some one moving about upstairs. The window was shoved up, and a protruding head said:

"What do you want?"

I replied: "I want to stay all night."

He said: "Who are you?"

I answered: "J. M. D. Burrows, of Davenport."

He replied: "Oh, yes, I've heard of you."

There was some whispering upstairs, after which he said: "Wait a few minutes; I will let you in."

Soon Daniel T. Newcomb appeared. I had never seen nor heard of him before, but that night was the beginning of a friendship that lasted until death ended it. I noticed, on my entrance, that I was in the home of a person of means and refinement. The surroundings were more luxurious than any I had seen in this new country. At daylight I was under way, and reached Muscatine soon after sunrise, which answered my purpose. I called on my way back, and renewed the acquaintance of the day before. I found Mr. Newcomb a very intelligent man, largely engaged in farming. He was opening more land than any one I had yet found. He was very enthusiastic, and spared neither labor nor money in his operations. He was a man of means, even in those days. He was the first to introduce labor-saving machinery in these parts—threshers, reapers, headers, etc.; and as I soon was engaged extensively in wheat-raising, I received a good deal of help and instruction as to handling and operating these implements. Mr. Newcomb always seemed to have a warm feeling for me. He raised more grain than any one else in this section, his one farm at Durant producing, one year, thirty thousand bushels, and he had so much confidence in me that he would sell his grain to no one else. This, in those primitive times, was a great help to me.

In 1842, when he bought the four-acre tract on Brady Street, Davenport, which Mrs. Newcomb continued to make her home after his death, he consulted me several times as to the wisdom of the purchase. A Mr. Perry had come here from Canada. His family was not satisfied, and wished to return to their old home. Mr. Perry owned eighty acres of land in East Davenport, since purchased by A. C. Fulton. Mr. Perry also owned the four-acre tract on Brady Street, and had put up a house on the lot at a cost of one thousand dollars. The house is still standing, in the rear of the First Presbyterian Church. Mr. Perry offered to sell the house and the four acres for twelve hundred dollars, which was considered the cheapest property in town. But there was no money, Mr. Newcomb being about the only man who held any of the "filthy lucre." He was a very cautious man, always thinking twice before acting. He intended to move to Davenport soon, but seriously questioned the prudence of investing so much money in four acres of land. I advised him to close the sale by all means, saying the property was cheap, and never would be worth less. He said he had not been fortunate in town-lot speculations. He had invested some in Camanche and Wapello, and some other places, which he regretted. He finally purchased the Brady-Street property. I think he got a reduction of one hundred dollars, which gave him the house and four acres for eleven hundred dollars.

Some years before his death he put up the comfortable and commanding residence, ever since known as the Newcomb Mansion. The view is enchanting. The noble Mississippi, the Island, Rock Island City, and a large part of Davenport, are spread out before you like a picture.

Mrs. Newcomb is a remarkable woman, of great business talent and judgment, and always has managed her large estate as well as any attorney could do for her. She is very liberal. She purchased several lots in Northwest Davenport, on which she erected the Newcomb Memorial Chapel, in memory of her husband. This she gave to the Presbyterian Church for a mission Sunday School. She also presented to the Academy of Sciences the lot now occupied by the Society,

besides contributing to many other chari-
table objects. Her private benefactions have
been numerous, and are known only to the
recipients. Although well advanced in years,
she is the same noble, queenly woman she
was when I first knew her, nearly fifty years
ago.

Chapter 14

IN 1843, produce was so low, and freight so high, on account of low water, that produce netted me a loss. I have spoken repeatedly of white beans in this book. At that early day there was a great demand for them, mostly for the Indians and the trading-posts above. The land was new and clean, and the farmers used to sow them broad-cast, the same as wheat. That year there was an unusual crop, and the quality was very superior. I had more than I knew what to do with, so thought I would try the New Orleans market. I put up one hundred barrels of the choicest white beans I ever saw. They were perfect—all of one size—and looked as if they had been cast in a mould. New Orleans was a good market for beans, they being needed for the negroes, and I made great calculations on my speculation, expecting to make a small fortune. The beans only cost me forty cents a bushel, and the barrels thirty-five cents each. Well, I

lost money on them; they did not sell for
enough to cover cost and transportation.
Such returns were not encouraging, either to
the farmer or to the merchant.

In the fall of 1843, as I said before, the low
prices and the high freight, caused by low
water, almost put a stop to navigation, and I
was subjected to constant loss in making my
fall shipments, so I resorted to an experi-
ment. I procured a first-class, A No. 1 keelboat[22] with a large cargo-box upon it. I never
saw a better or a safer one. It was as good
as a steamboat. I put in a heavy load, as
much as the state of the river would permit,
and hired a steamboat to tow her to St.
Louis, I assuming all expense of lightening at
the Lower Rapids. When I had sold out and
discharged my cargo in St. Louis, I loaded
her with my winter stock of goods, putting
in an unusual stock of salt, which article
was very scarce and high, that fall, in all our
river towns, on account of the low water.

[22] The keelboat was a long, narrow craft, built on a
keel and having a long cargo box. It was steered by a
special oar and propelled by poles, oars, and sails. A
footway on each side was provided for the use of the
crew in poling. Keelboats ran to 80 feet in length and
carried considerable cargoes of freight. They were in
common use on western rivers until after the Civil War.
See L. D. Baldwin, *The Keelboat Age on Western Waters*
(Pittsburgh, 1941).

The season was now getting pretty well advanced, and I was anxious to return, but could not get a boat to tow me for nearly a week. I at last secured one, the captain of which said he would tow me to Keokuk for certain, and to Davenport if he could get there, as he had freight to deliver between the Rapids. Before we reached Keokuk, the weather turned cold, and ice began to form. It took me two days to lighten up my barge. I finally got safely to Montrose, and loaded up again. In the meantime, the steamboat had been floundering on the Rapids, not able to get over. She at last gave it up, and I, after waiting another day, finding it growing colder, with no prospect of a boat from any quarter, hired a team, and, loading it up with goods, started for Davenport, leaving a crew of three good men whom I had brought with me. I instructed them to live in the boat and take good care of things until I could go home and send teams. The road was rough, but well frozen.

On reaching the Iowa River, it was very dark, and the ice not being considered very safe, I thought it imprudent to cross that night, as I knew the ice would be much stronger in the morning. There was a good farm-house at the crossing, and I ordered the teamster to put up for the night, and in the morning start for Davenport, but that I was going to Muscatine that night. I hired a horse and saddle of the man who was to keep the teamster, and promised to send it back when he returned. Just after I got safely over the river it began to rain heavily, and I do not think I ever experienced a colder rain. There were three or four inches of snow on the ground, and my horse's feet balled badly.

After I had made about five miles, the horse stumbled and fell, pitching me over his head. He got on his feet before I did, and would not let me catch him. After trying for some time, I had to give it up as a bad job, so abandoned him and shoved on afoot. A few miles farther on, I descended the bluff and struck Muscatine Island. There was a nice-looking house at the foot of the bluff, where I applied for shelter. The people informed me they could not keep me, but if I went half a mile farther, I would find good accommodations. About midnight I found the house, being almost perished with wet and cold and fatigue. I had no trouble to get accommodations, and the man of the house, renewing the fire, made me as comfortable as he could. Hanging my clothes by the fire to dry, I went to bed. Next morning, though it was still raining, I hired my host to hitch up his team and take me to Muscatine.

The first man I met there was a Davenporter, my friend William Van Tuyl.

I said: "Where on earth did you come from, Van?"

He said: "I came from Davenport this morning." It was then noon.

"When are you going back?" I asked.

He said: "It is such a bad day I shall not go until to-morrow."

I replied: "I must be in Davenport to-night, and I guess you'll have to take me."

He answered, laughingly: "As long as I can secure such good company, I guess I will."

After a good dinner we started, and by bed-time we were safe at home. It was Saturday night. I told Van Tuyl that I wanted twenty teams Monday morning to go to the Lower Rapids. He said to count him in for one—he would be on hand. During Monday, the team I had left at the Iowa River arrived. The teamster said when they got up in the morning, the first thing they saw was the horse I had hired. He was all right.

Monday morning, as soon as we could gather the teams, Mr. Prettyman, with his pockets full of money to pay expenses, and an escort of twenty-two wagons, at an expense of two dollars and fifty cents each and expenses paid, started for Montrose for the goods. The rain still continuing, the roads constantly became worse, until they were almost bottomless, and in many places on the bottoms the teams had to double to pull the empty wagons through. After a tedious time they arrived in Montrose. The men said it was useless to load up until the weather turned cool enough to freeze the ground, and as that was uncertain, Mr. Prettyman crossed over to Nauvoo, and asked the Mormon prophet, Joe Smith, what he would charge to tow the barge up with his steamboat, the *Nauvoo*. Smith said that as his boat was frozen up in a slough, it would be expensive getting her out, but finally agreed to tow the barge up for five hundred dollars. Prettyman told him to get his boat out as soon as possible, and sent the teams home, empty. The good steamer *Nauvoo*, with the barge, landed at our wharf about noon, the day before Christmas; the teams did not get back until two or three days later. The great expense we had been put to did not leave us much profit on our winter's business.

Chapter 15

Formation of the Firm of Burrows & Prettyman.—
More Low Water in the Mississippi.—Another Trip
by Flatboat to St. Louis.—Disastrous Journey to
New Orleans with a Cargo of Potatoes.

IN the spring of 1844, a Mr. Samuel
Fisher, living in Davenport and keeping
a store in Rock Island, offered Mr. Prettyman a half interest in his store if he would
take charge of it. Mr. Prettyman informed
me of the proposition. He said he did not
wish to leave me, but thought he ought to do
the best he could for himself. I said:

"Yes, a man ought to do what he thinks is
best for his own interest. You have been
clerking for me three years. We have never
had any disagreement. I should hate to part
with you; in fact, don't think I could get
along without you."

I added that I wished to think the matter
over for a few days, and would then decide.
I knew I could never get a man in whom I
could have such confidence as I had in Prettyman. No one could be more faithful and
honest. My business was increasing rapidly,
and I required not only competent help, but
plenty of it.

In a few days I told Mr. Prettyman that if he preferred to stay with me as my partner instead of going with Fisher, I had concluded he could do so; and that I had to go to Cincinnati and New Orleans to close out my winter accumulations of produce and lay in a spring supply for the store, which would take until the first of July. He accepted my proposition and became my partner; the firm of Burrows & Prettyman commencing July 1, 1844.

The low water, high freight, and extreme low prices ruling for produce that spring compelled me to again look around for some way to get my stuff to market without a sacrifice. I built the largest and best flat-boat that was ever at our landing, before or since. I loaded her with pork, bacon, lard, beans, oats, corn, and brooms. I also bought another good, strong boat, not so large, which I found at Le Claire, and loaded it entirely with potatoes, which were scarce and high that year. I loaded her with twenty-five hundred bushels, at fifty cents a bushel, New Orleans quotations being at that time two dollars a bushel. I sent my boats forward, with the intention of following and overtaking them before they reached St. Louis.

By inquiring of steamboats, I kept track of them, and when I thought they were near their destination, I started and overhauled them at about the mouth of the Illinois River. The captain of the boat I was on put me on board, and I went with them to the city. I did not offer my cargo for sale there, as it was intended for the New Orleans market. A party was anxious to buy my boat-load of potatoes, offering me fifty cents a bushel, and one hundred dollars for the boat, which was exactly what they had cost me at home; consequently, I did not sell. The New Orleans market quotations were still two dollars a bushel. My pilot said it would cost no more to take the two boats than one, as we could lash them together.

When I got ready to start, I found I could not get any insurance, as they were not in the habit of insuring flat-boats on the Upper Mississippi in those days. On the Ohio, a large business was done with flat-boats, and no trouble to get insurance; but St. Louis companies had not advanced that far. I did not dare to send them forward without insurance, as my capital was all there. After two days solicitation, through the influence of my friend, James E. Woodruff, who was one of the directors and a very influential man, the company agreed to take the risk if I would go with the boats and take charge of them in person. This changed all my arrangements. I had intended to see the boats safely off, and then return home, where I expected to remain a month before starting for New Orleans. Mr. Prettyman and my family expected me back in a week, and I wrote to them that I should be gone two months. We found the trip very tedious— had to lay up at night, and were often wind-bound two or three days at a time. When we reached Memphis, I thought I would try to sell my potatoes. I found there was no demand, the market being overstocked. Po-tatoes had been selling at two dollars a bushel, but the high price had induced such heavy shipments that the market was glut-ted, and the best offer I got was twenty-five cents a bushel; so I pulled out.

The next place was Vicksburg. The mar-ket there was no better, nor was it at Natchez. After six weeks, we arrived safely at New Orleans, to find a dull market—po-tatoes, no sale. The place was full of pota-toes, in willow hampers, from France. After a good deal of effort, I traded my whole cargo of potatoes to the captain of a Ber-muda vessel, at eight cents a bushel, delivered on board, which was just nothing at all, as it cost me all of that to sprout, barrel, and de-liver them; and I had to take coffee in pay-ment.

I soon sold out my other cargo, but at very low prices, and after buying a stock of goods at Cincinnati and St. Louis, for the new firm of Burrows & Prettyman, I set my face homeward.

Chapter 16

More Business Reverses in 1845.—The Rockingham
Mill Fiasco.—The Specious Boom in Wheat for
England.—The Boom Collapses.—Heavy Losses by
Burrows & Prettyman.—Our Transactions with
Henning & Woodruff.—Better Times Set In.

IN 1845, Rockingham having exploded,
and all her merchants withdrawn, and
her mill standing idle, I was induced to
lease the mill for two years, and also to put a
stock of goods there, which we placed in
charge of William Van Tuyl. The first year
we operated the Rockingham Mill was, I
think, the most disastrous I ever experienced. It was thought, in the fall of 1845,
and during the winter, that there was going
to be a large foreign demand for breadstuffs,
on account of a great deficiency in the English crops, and there was a great speculation
in breadstuffs in this country. At this time
we were doing business with the heaviest
produce house in the United States, com-
posed of Henning & Woodruff, of St. Louis,
John O. Woodruff & Co., of New Orleans,
and James E. Woodruff & Co., of New York
City,—it being all one house, and you could
ship to either branch you preferred. It was a

concern of unlimited means, and the senior partner, James E. Woodruff, was the best business friend I ever had, and he was also the best business man I ever knew.

When I first became acquainted with him, in 1842, they had not established their New York house, and he was the manager of the St. Louis establishment, where I made his acquaintance. He was a large operator. He thought there would be a large advance in the prices of breadstuffs before spring, to supply the deficiency in the English market, and wrote me repeatedly, urging me to buy every barrel of flour we could find, and all the wheat and other provisions, and that we were at liberty to draw on him for one hundred thousand dollars for that purpose. If we were afraid to buy on our own account, he said to buy for him. He urged us so strongly and persistently, that we followed his advice, buying on our own account. I visited every point, myself, as far as Dubuque, and bought every barrel of flour, and all the grain I could find, in New Albany, Savanna, Galena, and Dubuque, besides a large amount of provisions. We also sent an agent on the ice above Dubuque, to visit every point and buy all the flour and grain he could find in store. Consequently, at the opening of navigation we controlled the larger part of the produce in store above Davenport.

Then came trouble and disaster. The United States declared war against Mexico that spring, and everything collapsed. Prices tumbled more than one-half. The only way we could get to the seaboard was by the river to New Orleans, and by sea to New York, and the excitement then raging about privateers on the ocean almost suspended shipping. Insurance on the ocean advanced to ten per cent.

Soon after the opening of navigation, I began to move my winter accumulation, as I could see no prospect of any change for the better. I thought best to face the music at once. Our flour, in store on the river, had been bought at from four dollars to four dollars and fifty cents per barrel, and the wheat at an average of sixty cents a bushel. On arriving at St. Louis, the nominal price of flour was two dollars to two dollars and twenty-five cents a barrel, but no buyers; wheat, forty cents a bushel, for which there was a small local demand. Selling what wheat we could, we sent our flour and surplus wheat to New York, where it fared worse. Most of the flour became sour on the trip, and did not net us over one dollar per barrel, and wheat twenty-five cents a bushel.

When all was closed out, Burrows & Pretty-man found themselves nearly bankrupt. I do not think we could have paid over twenty-five cents on the dollar, if we had been forced to close up.

The first year of our Rockingham Mill operation did not leave us much courage for the next year's business; but as we had leased the mill for two years, we were compelled to run it. Our wheat crop for that year was good, but prices were ruinously low—wheat selling as low as twenty-five to thirty cents a bushel, and no money in it at that. When the fall trade commenced, and our farmers wanted to thresh, I found Mr. Prettyman badly demoralized. He thought we were ruined; said we had better let produce alone and stick to the store. This was the only time in our whole partnership that we differed in our business views. I did not blame him. I was as much disheartened as he was, but I knew our only salvation was in fighting our way through. After a few days of indecision, I said to Mr. Prettyman:

"The season is advancing, and our delay will ruin us. I do not want to force you to do what your judgment does not approve, but I have made up my mind. I am going to commence buying produce as usual, and will start up the mill. You are our book-keeper.

Charge all produce to my private account, with all expense of labor, etc. I will take the risk. Any other course would be suicidal."

That ended the matter, and he said:

"If you think it safe, and we can go on, it is all right."

We immediately sent word throughout the country that we would pay the highest prices for produce, half cash and half to be applied on debts or in payment for goods. Everything was low. We paid thirty cents a bushel for wheat, half cash and half goods and for debts, or where the party was compelled to have all money, we paid twenty-five cents a bushel, which, at the time, was more than it would net to ship to any other market.

We told our farmers we were hard up; that our means were all locked up in what they owed us, and urged them to pay up as promptly as possible. About this time I received a long letter from Woodruff, reviewing the situation. He had just arrived home from New York. He wrote me he was glad we were going to persevere, and believed we would soon retrieve all our losses. He thought the coming season would be successful; said that most of the dealers were broken up, and those who remained would buy at safe prices. He stated that E. K. Collins, a wealthy brother-in-law of his, a rich Quaker of New York City, the owner of that splendid line of ocean steamers, the Collins Line, running from New York to Liverpool, had promised him he would carry him through this crisis, and he added: "I am going to carry Billings, of Beardstown, on the Illinois River, Walker, of Burlington, and your firm through."

Well, everything went forward as usual. When we went to renew our fall stock of merchandise, Woodruff generously advanced us what we lacked to meet our fall payments; and, what was more, told me to be prudent, and as money was going to be very close that winter, and hard to get, not to use any more than I could help, but to buy anything I could see a profit on, and he would furnish the means. He also recommended that if we could manage to store what produce we had at home, not to ship any more until spring, as everything was so low that our fall freights left no margin. This advice made money for us, as everything in the spring was three times as high as in the fall.

Chapter 17

Retrieving the Ill-Luck of 1845.—A Big Speculation in
Wheat That Paid Enormous Profits.—The Rocking-
ham Corn Deal.—Corn a Glut in the Market.—
Selling Out Cheap.

DURING the winter, people began to
get over their scare of the previous
season, and a good foreign demand
springing up, prices, toward spring, began
to advance. Before the advance fairly began, Woodruff, foreseeing what was going to
happen, urged me to send out an agent at
once and buy everything I could above us,
and I did so, employing the same man that
I had the year before, Edward Davidson, a
first-rate business man. He bought largely.
People, remembering the disaster of the year
before, were willing sellers. About this time
hogs had begun to be so plenty, and we were
packing so extensively, that my winters
were occupied mostly overseeing that branch
of industry; so I was obliged to employ an
agent to make those trips abroad.

One bitter cold, stormy day, about the
first of February, there was nothing doing;
no farmers in town, and I was tired of sitting
around the stove. I put on my overcoat, and

said to Mr. Prettyman, "I will go out and try to buy what wheat there is in town."

I first called on Charles Lesslie, at the corner of Front and Brady streets. He had a small warehouse full of very choice wheat, mostly raised by the Brownlies, at Long Grove, who, at that time, were considered the best farmers in the county. After considerable talk, I bought him out. I agreed to pay him sixty cents a bushel, and to take the wheat away any time I pleased between then and the 1st of May, and pay for it when removed. There were about twenty-five hundred bushels. Soon afterward, in April, I sold the lot to a St. Louis speculator for one dollar and twenty-five cents a bushel. All the expense I had was to sack the wheat and deliver it to the boat, the buyer to furnish the sacks.

I then called on William Inslee and bought what he had, paying the same price, and he had about the same amount. Whisler then occupied the lot at the corner of Front and Main streets, and had a large warehouse, which, as he was a large dealer, was pretty well filled. I also bought him out, paying the same price.

This closed out all the wheat in town. I went back to the store well satisfied with my forenoon's work. As I afterwards sold it for double what I paid for it, we made about five thousand dollars in the operation.

We found, at the opening of navigation, that we had on hand a larger supply of breadstuffs than any other person on the river. The profits on flour made in the fall and held over, and that made from thirty-cent wheat, bought in the early part of the winter, was simply enormous—flour costing us two dollars a barrel, selling for seven dollars. As we could well afford to sell, in the spring we put our stuff on the market as rapidly as possible, and by July I had paid every dollar we owed, and had money to our credit in the hands of Henning & Woodruff, with which, as we did not need it, we proposed to put up a flouring mill in Davenport. The town thus far had neither a flour mill nor a saw-mill. We intended to give her both, which I will refer to hereafter.

The first year we operated the Rockingham Mill, 1845, there being a large surplus of corn, to accommodate our customers living in the southern part of the county, we purchased a large quantity, to be delivered at Rockingham, paying ten cents a bushel. We filled every empty dwelling-house in the place—and there were a good many, the inhabitants having left the town in her adversity. Burrows & Prettyman, while they opposed Rockingham in her prosperity, stood by her in her last days, and were the last to operate her mill, and sold the last goods in her territory.

The price of corn, in the spring, would not permit our transporting it to any market, the cost of the gunny-bags and freight being more than the corn would bring. There was one house we were compelled to vacate on the first of June, as the owner wanted to remove it to Davenport. As we could not ship it, we sold it to a farmer, George Hawley, of Pleasant Valley (one thousand bushels, at eight cents a bushel), and took an old horse in payment, at eighty dollars. Hawley hauled the corn to his farm for feed, it being cheaper than he could raise it.

Such were the dangers and difficulties of the produce business the first eight years in Iowa.

Chapter 18

Advent of the Germans in Davenport.—A Sturdy and
Industrious Race.—Outbreak of the Cholera.—Many
Fatal Cases.—To St. Louis Overland.—Hard Traveling on the Home Trip.—Some Facetious Young Men,
and Who Laughed Last.—Seasons of Hard Work.

ABOUT this time there was a prospect
of brighter days. Our German fellow-citizens began to come to Davenport in large numbers, and many of them
possessed a good deal of money, which the
country sadly needed. They entered large
tracts of land, which they immediately improved.

This year the cholera prevailed in Davenport, and many of the German immigrants
had ship-fever among them. They came by
the way of New Orleans; every steamboat
landing at our wharf left some. There was
much excitement on account of the cholera.
Many of our best citizens were dying. A
man would be well at bed-time, and dead before morning. Many immigrants could not
get shelter, and Burrows & Prettyman
threw open their porkhouse and warehouse
for use until the immigrants could put up
shanties on the prairie. Many men, now

wealthy farmers, occupied our buildings until they could do better; among these I remember M. J. Rohlfs, since then Treasurer of Scott County for ten years; also N. J. Rusch, afterward State Senator, and Lieutenant Governor of Iowa. I always have had a warm feeling for the Germans for their help in settling up Scott County, when help was so much needed. It is astonishing to see what they have accomplished. You can find scarcely a German farmer who is not wealthy. The banks of Davenport contain about six millions of deposits (which, I believe, is as much as all the rest of the State claims to have), and half of the money is owned by Germans.

In the fall of 1845, after navigation was closed on the river, I found it would be necessary for me to go to St. Louis. Prettyman said our sales had been large, and we would be out of many leading articles before spring, and if I could manage to get them here, he wished I would buy some. I told him to make up a list of dry goods such as he needed, about a good wagon-load, and I would bring them up.

I went over to Beardstown, on the Illinois River, by stage, and down the Illinois and Mississippi rivers by steamboat, to St. Louis. In St. Louis, after my business was transacted, I purchased Mr. Prettyman's bill of goods, and shipped them by the river to Keokuk, as the boat was to go no farther. We did not get there on account of ice, but the boat landed us four miles below, at a small town called Warsaw, on the Illinois shore.

When we left St. Louis it was dark, and I did not see any one I knew on the boat. The first thing I did in the morning, after breakfast, was to take a walk on the guards to get fresh air. I soon heard familiar voices on the deck below, and on going down, saw seven young men from Pleasant Valley, customers of ours, among whom I can only remember George Hawley and two of the Fenno boys. They had been down to St. Louis with two flat-boats loaded with onions, and were then in a dilemma as to how they were to get home. They wanted to know what I was going to do. I told them I should hire a team to haul my goods, and would ride on the wagon. When the boat landed us, I found and hired a team. The boys wanted me to let them put on their baggage. The teamster said it would overload us; but they were so anxious, and being good customers of ours, I told the teamster if he would carry their baggage I would walk with the men.

We reached Carthage, the county-seat, at noon, and stopped and got dinner, by which time a heavy storm of rain and sleet set in. The men wanted to lay over until the next day, but I insisted upon pushing on; so we all put out during the afternoon and traveled until dark, when we put up at a farmhouse. I overheard the boys, in the afternoon, saying I could not stand it long—that they would soon have "my hide on the fence." I thought to myself, "We will see."

We started out next morning in a snowstorm, calculating to make Monmouth that night. When we got within five or six miles of that place the men began to give out, saying they could travel no farther. George Hawley and myself were the only ones to get through, which we did about nine o'clock that night. I hired the landlord to send out a two-horse wagon and pick up the other men and bring them in. He found them scattered along the road for miles, completely exhausted. I said nothing, but wondered whose hides ornamented the fence.

The next day we arrived home safely, having walked the whole distance in a heavy storm, all travel-worn, sore, and weary. It was about as hard a trip as the one I made from Prairie du Chien to Dubuque, some years before.

I had been packing considerable pork for a few years, and I sold it mostly to the Fur

Company [23] and to parties filling Indian contracts. The wheat I handled, from 1840 to 1845, that I did not get made into flour, I bought on commission for a large mill in Cincinnati—C. S. Bradbury & Co.

Our business had now (1847) become well established, large amounts of produce coming in from the counties of Cedar, Linn, Jones, Clinton, and Jackson.

Our store was well patronized, and we hardly ever closed it until midnight. In the forenoons, the farmers in our county, from the Groves and points within a circuit of ten or fifteen miles, would come in with their grain, etc., and by the time they had unloaded and done their trading, another section would begin to arrive from Clinton and Cedar Counties and the territory still farther distant—a big day's travel—and would not all get in until near bedtime. They wanted to

[23] The American Fur Company was incorporated in 1808 for a twenty-five year period. By consolidations, absorptions, and cut-throat competition it eventually disposed of almost all rivals, and by about the year 1828 it practically monopolized the fur trade of the United States. Changing conditions led to its ultimate downfall; John J. Astor, its founder, withdrew in 1833, and in 1842 the great company failed. It was subsequently reorganized as a commission house, and the author's dealings with it apparently belong to this later period of its existence.

unload and do their trading, so as to start home early next morning, that they might reach home the same day. This made our business very laborious.

Chapter 19

IN July, 1842, A. C. Fulton made his
appearance in Davenport. He possessed
great activity and energy, and was a
good citizen in his way; but many of his
early ventures did not indicate an aptness
for mercantile life. He brought with him a
bankrupt stock of dry goods, etc. purchased
in New Orleans. They were as heterogene-
ous a lot of articles as ever were landed in
the town. He told me at the time that they
were bankrupt goods, and that when he
purchased them, instead of having them in-
voiced, as customary, he had taken them in
a lump, at "so much for what is on this
side of the house, and so much for that side,"
and so on. A great deal of the stuff was un-
salable. It was said that in the stock were
two barrels of fish-hooks—enough to supply
the Davenport trade for one hundred years.
After Mr. Fulton had sold what goods he

could, not wishing or not being able to renew his trade, Burrows & Prettyman bought him out, paying about two thousand dollars, and mixed the goods in their stock.

Mr. Fulton had arrived in Davenport in the latter part of July. After opening his goods in a small room at Second and Rock Island streets, he immediately announced to the suffering inhabitants that goods were twenty-five to thirty per cent too high, and produce twenty-five to thirty per cent too low. Of course, that was good news to the inhabitants, and brought Mr. Fulton into notice with a jump. He at once pitched into the onion crop, then growing. He said he would contract for the onions at fifty cents a bushel. We had not been in the habit of contracting for onions at any price, but generally bought at the market value, which then ruled at twenty to twenty-five cents a bushel.

Mr. Fulton's attempt to boom the onion market caused dissatisfaction. Our customers wanted to know why we could not pay more than half as much for onions as Mr. Fulton did. We told them we were willing to allow them all we could get for the onions, but were not disposed to follow such a reckless leader. We advised them to contract their onions at fifty cents, which most of them did; but the trouble was, they had to have money to meet their engagements to our firm and to other merchants, and they could get only goods from Mr. Fulton

Mr. Stephen Henley, of Pleasant Valley, one of our best customers and a very estimable man, had a large crop of onions. Mr. Fulton offered him fifty cents; we offered twenty-five. Henley had to have the money for his crop. He felt sore about our paying but half what Mr. Fulton offered him, and we agreed to ship the onions for him on his own account, if he preferred, and to furnish the bags, and charge him nothing for our trouble, beyond the price of the bags and the amount paid for labor, etc. Henley brought in the onions, and we shipped them. The result was that they made a loss for him, not selling for enough to pay for sacks, freight, and charges.

When the onion crop came in, Mr. Fulton, not having any warehouse, had the onions unloaded in the yard, and upon open lots, and the little village was soon fragrant with decaying onions.

As every family kept one cow or more, a great cry arose about the flavor of the milk, and Mr. Fulton became very unpopular with the housewives during the onion season.

But how those onions rolled in! It seems that Mr. Fulton had kept no account of his contracts, and people imposed upon him, bringing more than he ever bought—not only their own crops, but those of their neighbors and friends. Mr. Fulton's investment in onions was practically a total loss. He loaded a flat-boat with some of the best of the luscious fruit, in October, but the boat froze in before it reached Burlington (our river closing that year on the 17th of November), and the boat lay there until the latter part of April, by which time the onions were worthless.

Mr. Fulton did not arrive in Davenport until late in July, yet he managed not only to monopolize the onion crop of that year, at heavy losses to himself and the natives, but also, with the help of two other ingenious and imaginative gentlemen, to dam the Wapsipinicon that winter, and build a mill and warehouse—at least, verbally, and with all the enthusiasm of Colonel Mulberry Sellers in grid-ironing Central Asia with imaginary railroad systems.

Buchanan County, where this great feat of imagination was accomplished, had only about fifty inhabitants. Yet Mr. Fulton, that year, furnished them a mammoth mill and warehouse, or rather the glowing plans for them. He did not do this for Davenport until five years later.

Mr. Fulton not only revolutionized the prices of produce and merchandise in Davenport, dammed the Wapsipinicon, and built the mill and warehouse, but he also conceived the practicability of leading the waters of the Mississippi River, at the Upper Rapids, by canal along the Iowa shore, and creating a water-power for mills and factories. For the fulfillment of this grand work of genius and engineering, civil engineers were engaged at great expense, and a survey of the proposed gigantic artificial waterway was made. Besides this, Mr. Fulton purchased Smith's Island, and numerous strips of land one hundred feet wide, bordering on the river, for his canal. After all these elaborate and costly preliminaries, his money gave out, and the project was found to be an undertaking just a little too heavy for one man. All further work on the canal was abandoned, and the property was sold at a sacrifice.

I must, although it is not within my fifty years' experience, refer to a little matter that amused me when I read it. I would not mention it, were the story not so much like Mr. Fulton's first year's operations here. In the Biographical Dictionary, written or dictated by himself, he says:

During 1835, Santa Anna, Dictator of Mexico, issued a proclamation, requiring all Americans to leave Texas.

He increased his army, and marched forth to enforce his demand. Mr. Fulton, though quite a young man at the time, called upon the friends of oppressed Texas, through the press, to join him, and march to the rescue. The immediate result was that a volunteer corps of over three hundred young men was formed, which was the main force at the victorious battle of the Mission, and the storming and capture of the fortified town of Baxar, which caused the withdrawal of all Mexican troops from the State; and Mr. Fulton's undertaking was crowned with success; which act eventually gave us Texas and California, and changed the destiny of this Union.

Mr. Fulton's achievements in Davenport in 1842, and the greater feat of conquering Santa Anna, I have never seen or heard equaled, unless it be in the history of the astonishing exploits of Don Quixote.[24]

[24] The sketch of Fulton's career which the author quotes is in the *History of Scott County, Iowa* (Chicago, 1882), 835–39. He was born in Chester County, Penn., in 1811, and according to the sketch was a relative of Robert Fulton of early steamboat fame. At the time the county history was published he was still living in Davenport. It seems evident that he did not lack self-assurance or a due appreciation of his achievements. The historians of Texas whom the present writer has consulted give no space to Fulton's supposed contributions to the early history of that commonwealth.

Chapter 20

Mr. Fulton's Peculiar Manner of Dealing in Mill Property.—A Rivalry with Some Bitterness.—Failure of the Opposition Mill.—Mr. Fulton's Serious Illness.—A Sick-Bed Reconciliation.

IN 1847, Burrows & Prettyman, having been very successful that year at milling in Rockingham, concluded to build a flouring-mill and a saw-mill in Davenport. Our idea was to put the engine-house in the middle, the flour-mill on one side and the saw-mill on the other; and to run the saw-mill in the day-time and the grist-mill at night, as we feared there was not wheat enough raised here to run a flour-mill steadily.

Mr. Fulton was putting up a large brick building at the foot of Perry Street, on the bank of the river, near our store, which he said was for a mill. In the spring it was nearly finished and ready for the machinery, which was the most expensive part of the undertaking, and required ready money, and, for a first-class mill, plenty of it. Mr. Fulton had heard of a flour-mill in Pittsburgh which was going to be dismantled, the machinery of which was for sale. He went to

Pittsburgh, intending to buy the machinery, but not having the money, and being unable to offer such security as was satisfactory, he returned without the machinery, and his mill scheme thus proved as big a failure as his canal had proved, a few years before.

A few days after he returned, Mr. Fulton called on me, and said he understood we were going to build a mill. We told him we thought of it.

Mr. Fulton said: "You had better buy my building. I cannot finish it, and there is not wheat enough raised for two mills."

Mr. Prettyman and myself thought the matter over, and we decided to drop the saw-mill part of our project, and turn our attention to putting up a first-class steam flouring-mill. His building was on the very ground we wanted, and, with a few alterations, would answer our purpose; so we decided to buy the building, if we could agree on the price. He asked four thousand dollars. We finally settled on three thousand seven hundred and fifty dollars.

We employed William H. Gayl to put in the machinery. Mr. Gayl was considered the best millwright in the West, having fitted out some of the finest mills in the country, and we set him to work as soon as we could obtain his services.

Just at this point Mr. Fulton took a step which was productive of some unpleasantness. In his *History of Scott County*, he has this to say in extenuation of his conduct:

"The citizens and farmers expressed great sorrow that he [Mr. Fulton] had sold the mill, and called on him by a committee to express their feelings."

He replied: "Get the owner of the adjacent ground to sell to me at a fair value, and I will erect another mill and operate it."

"When shall we say to the owner that you will begin work?" Mr. Fulton says the committee asked him.

He was in such haste to start this new scheme, directly in violation of his agreement with Burrows & Prettyman, that he replied: "I will begin to-morrow morning."

He could make that Napoleonic answer at that particular time, because he had in his pocket three thousand seven hundred and fifty dollars of Burrows & Prettyman's money, with which to buy machinery. It was easy enough to put up a frame building in the way of trade and barter, but it took money to buy machinery, and he had our money to do it with. He secured the ground adjoining our mill, and put up a hastily constructed pine building, immediately alongside, which increased our rate of insurance almost double, putting us to the extra expense of some three or four hundred dollars a year, for several years.

This naturally did not tend to strengthen our business friendship, and I vowed to myself that Mr. Fulton's mill never should make him any money.

Both mills were started the next winter, Mr. Fulton's about three days before ours. We did not start up until our mill was finished and ready for business, and had no stoppage for alterations, while our neighbor was more or less troubled for several days. The mills were finished, and run strong opposition. "War to the knife, and the knife to the hilt," was our motto.

Burrows & Prettyman had the best mill, at that day, in the State of Iowa, turning out more flour, and better, than any other. We also had the best miller in the State, Hiram Johnson. He superintended our milling for thirteen years. Our brand, Albion Mills, soon became well known, and brought, in the open market, fifty cents a barrel more than any spring wheat flour made above St. Louis. We built our mill to be run night and day, and as we could not get a supply of wheat at home, we established agencies up the river, at Princeton, Camanche, New Albany, Lyons, and other points.

We had boat-load after boat-load taken in for us in a large barn in a corn-field where Clinton now stands—no Clinton then.[25] We chartered a small steamboat, called the *Oneota*, put on her a crew of our own, and kept her busy boating wheat to our mill.

To obviate the difficulty in getting wheat at harvest time, when it was always scarce for a few weeks before the farmers began to thresh, I, myself, began to raise wheat, and grew from one thousand to eighteen hundred acres, year after year. Meanwhile, I kept the price of wheat in Davenport high enough to keep Mr. Fulton from making any money, knowing that when I barely paid expenses, he was running at a loss.

Mr. Fulton soon ran his career at milling. He involved himself so that there were some

[25] In 1836 Joseph M. Bartlett "squatted" on the site of present-day Clinton and projected an extensive town which he modestly named New York. In 1838 he sold his claim (including a fancied gold deposit) to Messrs. Pearce, Randall, and Jennings, and by the autumn of 1840 sixteen voters cast their ballots in the first election of the new settlement. The real birth of the modern city, however, occurred in 1855 when the Iowa Land Company laid out a town-site and persuaded the North-western Railroad Company to cross the Mississippi here instead of at nearby (and slightly older) Lyons. The location of the railroad line insured the future of Clinton and at the same time doomed Lyons to a rôle of permanent inferiority to its down-river neighbor.

thirty-odd suits pending in the District Court against him at one time. In the *Biographical Dictionary*, speaking of these two mills, he says, after remarking that he sold the first building to Burrows & Prettyman, who completed it "and put it in successful operation," that "his mill, as a financial operation, proved a failure, as almost every shipment resulted in a loss."

When Mr. Fulton could operate his mill no longer, he succeeded in leasing it to George L. Davenport, William Inslee, and Louis Macklot, who ran it one or two years, suffering a great loss, which they were abundantly able to stand, as it was a strong firm. We always were on good terms with every one of the firm, our opposition being only fair business competition, and a determination on my part that that mill never should make anything—and it never did.

During the latter part of Davenport, Inslee & Macklot's lease, Mr. Fulton was taken dangerously sick with typhoid fever. For some time he was not expected to live. People would say to me: "They say Fulton is going to die."

One day, one of the family came to the store, and left word that Mr. Fulton would like to see me. I went. I shall never forget that interview. Mr. Fulton lived in a cozy brick house, at Second and Perry streets, on the ground now occupied by Nicholas Kuhnen's tobacco factory. He was in bed, in a room on the first floor. When I entered, he put out his hand, and I took it. We had not shaken hands or spoken to each other for three years.

Mr. Fulton asked me to be seated. I inquired as to the state of his health. He said: "I've been getting better for a few days. Last week I thought I would be in the bone-yard before this."

I never had heard the expression "bone-yard," and it struck me as singular. He continued:

"Since I have been sick and lying here, I have been thinking over our difficulties, and I am satisfied that I have been to blame in the matter. You had good reason to believe, when you bought me out, that I would not build another mill. But I injured myself more than I did you; it ruined me."

I at once replied: "If you feel that way, Mr. Fulton, say no more; it is wiped out."

Since then, we always have been friends. Our paths have not crossed each other.

Chapter 21

Burrows & Prettyman Buy the Ætna Mill.—Mr.
Fulton's Successful Real Estate Operations.—A
Commercial Sensation.—Wreck of the Ætna Mill.—
The Purchase of Offermann's Island, and Its Subsequent Sale.—Some Reverses.

SOON after Mr. Fulton got well, he went
into the real estate business, which he
understood, and understands, and which
has made him one of the solid men of Davenport.

The Mr. Perry whose name is mentioned
in a foregoing chapter as interested in the
four-acre lot which D. T. Newcomb bought,
died before he sold the eighty acres in East
Davenport. Mr. Fulton got on the track,
somehow—found his heirs, I believe, in
Canada—and bought the tract at a very low
price, and attached it as an addition to our
city. It has been pretty well built over, and
has made his fortune.

As soon as Mr. Fulton was able to attend to
business, he called on me, wishing to sell his
mill to us. I told him he must think me deranged to consider such a proposition. "What
do we want of two mills?" said I. "Our own
mill never has made any money for us yet."

Said Mr. Fulton: "You can make money by buying my mill and letting it lie idle." He added: "How much wheat do you grind in a year? Do you grind a hundred thousand bushels a year?"

Said I: "Yes, and more."

He said: "Do you not pay five cents a bushel more than you would if it were not for that mill?"

I said: "Yes, we pay full five cents more than it is worth."

"Then," said he, "you would save five thousand dollars a year, if you bought my mill and let it lie idle."

"Even if we wanted to buy," I answered, "we could not spare the money. We have not made anything the past two years, and our means are all locked up."

Mr. Fulton said he believed he could sell the mill to us without a dollar down, and that he would rather sell it to me than to any other man living. He thought he could use our notes, made payable at such times as we could save it from the price of wheat.

About two weeks later, Mr. Fulton told me he had heard from his creditors, and that they would take our notes. Meanwhile we had thought the matter over, and concluded it would be cheaper to buy the mill, and let it lie idle, than to fight it. Consequently, we purchased the property, paying ten thousand seven hundred and fifty dollars, in notes of twenty-five hundred dollars each, payable every six months, until all should be paid.

This was the third large transaction I had with Mr. Fulton. I first bought his stock of goods; then the mill building for our first mill; and, finally, his other mill. In each transaction, I had acted rather from compulsion than from business preference; and all three transactions proved obstacles in my career. When we purchased his last mill, the Ætna, the gentlemen operating it still had two months to run before their lease expired; but the sale of the mill was known to the seller and buyers only, until after the lease run out. They gave up the mill at night, and we took possession the next morning, raised steam, and set her to work, with our flag flying. There was a sensation in the town when it became known that Burrows & Prettyman had gobbled up both mills. It created a small commercial cyclone, and some opposition spirits tried to start a project for a third mill, saying that Burrows & Prettyman were monopolizing all the business, and would give no one else a chance. Well, the cyclone soon expended itself, as wind flurries generally do.

We tried running the mill for some time, but found we could make more money by letting it lie idle. We used it for a warehouse for several years.

One year, we had an unusual stock of pork and grain. We put up, that season, nineteen thousand hogs, and were very much pinched for storage room. We used, that winter, the lower story of the Ætna Mill for packing pork, and the two and a half stories above were filled to the roof with corn, oats, barley, rye, and mill-stuffs.

Early in March we had a three-day blizzard. On the last day (a Sunday), the building collapsed. The flooring on every story looked as if it had been sawed off, it was broken so clean and even at the sides. We found out, in clearing away the debris, that the pillars in the cellar, sustaining the building, which were made of brick, had crumbled, thus letting the floors down. Our grain was somewhat mixed, and caused us considerable expense and labor in properly separating and taking care of it.

As the building was now fit for neither a mill nor a warehouse, we traded the inside, or machinery, to Adrian H. Davenport, of Le Claire, for Credit Island,[26] now called

[26] Credit Island, now known as Suburban Island, lies on the Iowa side of the Illinois-Iowa boundary, within

Offermann's Island. He took the machinery to Le Claire, and used it to put in a mill which was eventually burned. We cut two thousand cords of wood from the island, when, finding it a good deal of trouble to take care of, as our timber was constantly being stolen, we sold the island to Josiah Jenny, for three thousand dollars. He sold it to old Mr. Gilruth, the Methodist preacher; he sold it to Mr. Offermann, who sold it to some company in Chicago, and it is now used, in summer, as picnic and pleasure grounds.

the city limits of Davenport. Here, on Sept. 5, 1814, Major Zachary Taylor (later President of the United States) and his command of 334 men in 8 keelboats suffered a defeat at the hands of 30 British soldiers equipped with 3 small cannon, and supported by 1000 or more Sauk and Fox warriors. This is said to have been the only battle of the War of 1812 fought west of the Mississippi, and the only battle ever fought on Iowa soil in which British regular soldiers participated. For an account of it see Wm. A. Meese, "Credit Island, 1814–1914" in *Journal* of the Ill. State Hist. Society, VII, 349–73. The unexpected triumph of the British was chiefly due to the remarkable skill of a single gunner, Sergeant James Keating. For the story of his exploit see M. M. Quaife, "A Forgotten Hero of Rock Island." *Ibid.*, XXIII, 652–63.

Chapter 22

History of the Banking Business in Davenport.—Cook
& Sargent's Early Operations.—Currency Very
Scarce and Unsafe.—The Loss of a Trunk Filled with
Bullion, and Its Recovery.—Hard Times in a Stage-
Coach.—Lost in an Old-Fashioned Blizzard.

I STILL had to go frequently to St. Louis,
after our river closed. In those days,
three times as many steamboats were
run on the Illinois River as now, and they
ran, generally, three weeks later in the fall,
and began running two weeks earlier in the
spring, than on the Upper Mississippi. I
often went by stage to Beardstown, and
by way of the Illinois River to St. Louis.

Cook & Sargent began a banking business
in 1847. Our currency was very unsafe, and
gold and silver and eastern bank bills were
at a large premium over our western circulation. There was a large private banking
house in Philadelphia—Clark & Brothers—
with a branch in New York (Clark, Dodge &
Co.), and one in St. Louis (Clark & Brothers). They supplied a large share of the circulation in this section. The Philadelphia
house would draw on the St. Louis house,
say, for one dollar or five dollars. They

Fifty Years in Iowa

(Clark & Brothers) would accept the draft, which, of course, would be payable at their St. Louis house. Merchants considered it safer than our western banks, as the credit of the house of Clark & Brothers was A No. 1, but could not be used for eastern exchange without a large discount, being, as I have explained, payable in St. Louis.

I was about to make a trip to St. Louis, when Ebenezer Cook called on me, and asked me if I would take a package of gold (twenty-six hundred dollars) down for them, and bring ten thousand dollars currency back. I told him I would. This was before we had express companies, as we have now. We used then to carry trunks instead of grip-sacks.

Cook & Sargent sent their package of gold over to the store, and I put it in my trunk. I started from Rock Island in the stage: traveled all that day and night for Beardstown. My trunk was tied on behind. A rope ran through the handles, and the ends were tied at each side to a standard. There was nothing to hold the trunk there except the rope. The roads were very rough, and I felt uneasy for the safety of my valuable baggage.

The stage was a regular old "mud-stage," and had no covered boot,[27] to protect the

[27] The boot on the stagecoaches of the period, was an enclosed compartment in the rear of the body of the

trunk from getting wet or being stolen. I did not fear so much for its being lost, as that it might be stolen. The stage carried the mail, and had to stop at every town and get the mail changed. I got out whenever we stopped, and looked to see if my trunk was all right.

Some time before daylight, when within ten miles of Beardstown, I got out at the post-office, as usual, when, to my consternation, I discovered that my trunk was gone.

I ran to the driver, and told him some one had stolen my trunk. We examined, and found that it had not been stolen, but that the handles, from the constant pitching and plunging over the bad roads and chuck-holes, had pulled out. I told the driver I should go back as far as the last post-office.

There was only one livery-stable in the place. I routed out the owner, and asked him to hitch up a team at once, declaring that it was important for me to go over the road before daylight, and that it would take a smart team to do it. He owned only four or five old, broken-down horses; but I saw a

coach, tapering to a junction with the body at its top. In a rough way it may be likened to the present-day enclosed trunk compartments at the rear end of passenger automobiles. Earlier stagecoaches, like earlier automobile bodies, lacked such a compartment.

very good-looking span of horses and a light rig in the stable, and I said to him: "Why not take these?" He said they were not his. I told him if he would let me have them, I would give him five dollars, whether we had to go one mile or the whole seven.

It took the liveryman a good while to get ready, but, after starting, we made double-quick time.

When we had driven about five miles, I saw something black in the road, half a mile ahead. I said to the driver: "There it is;" and when we reached the black object, which proved to be the trunk, the sun was just rising. There was a farm-house not ten rods away, and the people were just getting up.

We returned over the road about as quickly as we had come, and got a good breakfast, after which I hired the liveryman to take me to Beardstown, where I took a steamer for St. Louis.

On my return from St. Louis, after leaving Beardstown in the stage, a big snow-storm of the regulation blizzard style set in, and we were stalled. It was storming terribly when we stopped at a farm-house, at three o'clock P. M., for dinner. After dinner, about four o'clock, we again started out. The roads were all snowed under, and the wind blew a gale. As there were no fences to show where the road lay, our driver lost his bearings and began to drive at random. We could not find any house.

About midnight we got mired in a slough. There were some five or six of us in the stage. We got out and helped the driver, but with all our efforts we could not extricate ourselves. After an hour's exertion we gave it up, and, all but exhausted, crawled back into the stage to keep from freezing, while the driver started off to seek assistance. An hour later, he returned with a farmer and a span of horses. They pulled us through, and at two o'clock in the morning we arrived at the farm-house, which was a mile from where we had been stuck, and only three miles from the place where we had taken dinner the day before. We had been driving around, almost in a circle, for ten hours, and made but three miles!

The next morning, as the storm continued, the driver did not think it safe to start out, so we stayed until after dinner, when our host, with his team, helped us to the next post-office station, where we stopped all night. The next day we reached home, after a three days' trip, when we should have made the journey in a trifle more than one day.

Chapter 23

Change in the Firm of Burrows & Prettyman.—Young
Edward Davidson's Service.—Trading Up and Down
the River.—Success of the New Business Scheme.

PREVIOUS to this time, Burrows &
Prettyman had employed for five or six
years, every winter, a young man, Edward Davidson, whom we kept on the ice
with a horse and sleigh, between Dubuque
and St. Paul, running back and forth to purchase grain. Prettyman and myself hardly
ever went home from the store before midnight, being engaged in writing up the books
and straightening up the goods. When
Davidson was in town he often stayed at the
store until we closed up. One night I overheard Mr. Prettyman and he talking about
his buying Prettyman's interest in the firm.
I thought at first it was only talk—that
neither of them was speaking seriously; but
there was so much of this talk, from time to
time, that, one evening, when Mr. Prettyman
and I were in the store alone, I said to him:

"How is it about you and Davidson? Are
you really in earnest in what you say about
selling out?"

He said he was. I told him that was something I had to be consulted about; I could not allow him to choose a partner for me. I told him Mr. Davidson was a very estimable young man, but I did not want him for a partner. I inquired of Mr. Prettyman what the trouble was. He said there was no trouble, except that he did not like the produce business. There was too much hard work, and too much risk; that we had made nothing for two years, and had worked like slaves. He said our store had grown to large proportions, and he believed if we let produce alone and devoted our entire attention to the store, we would do better than to do so much other business. I told him that, even if we were disposed to do so, we could not. We had the mill, pork-house, and warehouse on our hands, could not sell them, and must use them. I said:

"The matter is easily arranged. You like selling goods; I do not. You take the store; I will take the mill, pork-house, etc."

This did not suit him. He wanted to sell out his interest in the produce operations only, but desired me to keep a half interest in the store.

Well, after a good deal of thought and deliberation, we arranged our business on the following basis: I retained a half interest in the store, and bought the mill, warehouse, pork-house, and cooper-shop, giving Burrows & Prettyman my note for thirty thousand dollars, payable in five years, at ten per cent interest, with a verbal understanding that I could pay it before if I could make the money; but at the end of the time specified, I would pay it, if I had to sell property to do it. I also told Mr. Prettyman that my own individual business would occupy my time, and anything I did for the store would be as a volunteer. Although I expected to be able to do as much as I had been doing, I thought I ought to do something more, to offset his services. The book-keeper drew the highest wages of any one we employed. I told Mr. Prettyman he could hire any book-keeper he desired, and charge his wages to my private account. Our bank account was to be kept in the name of Burrows & Prettyman, they paying for all grain, labor, etc., and charging the same to my account; and, in return, all the debts of Burrows & Prettyman, as they fell due, were to be paid by J. M. D. Burrows and credited to his account.

On the first day of each month, the book-keeper made out a balance-sheet, and Mr. Prettyman gave Burrows & Prettyman's note for whatever balance they owed.

Chapter 24

Edward Davidson's Business Venture.—Trips Along the River.—His Death in Trying to Cross on Moving Ice.—Operations of Burrows & Prettyman.—Some Successful Investments.—Sale of the Pork-House.

EDWARD DAVIDSON, to whom I have before referred, operated for me on the river a number of years more, until our own crops were so abundant that they produced all I wanted, and I did not need to send abroad; so I abandoned my old winter operations above Dubuque. This disappointed the young man. He had been expecting to operate for me, as usual. He said he believed he would try it on his own account, if I would give him letters, which I did. I wrote to Henning & Woodruff, and others in St. Louis, and to grain points above, recommending Davidson as a man of superior business habits and honesty. It was pretty late before he got off.

On his return trip, he arrived at McGregor's Landing,[28] on the Iowa shore, late one

[28] McGregor's Landing, on the Iowa shore of the Mississippi opposite Prairie du Chien, Wis., was long known as McGregor and in more recent years as Marquette. Before the Chicago, Milwaukee and St. Paul

afternoon. He inquired how the crossing
was, and was informed that it was not considered very safe. He said he wished to go
over to Prairie du Chien, but would like to
have supper before starting; he would leave
his horse and cutter until morning, and go
over on foot. After supper, just about dusk,
he started over. Next day he did not return,
which made the landlord anxious, especially
as the river, during the night, had become
more unsafe than the day before.

That night the ice moved, and next day it
started down stream. It was not until then
that there was any crossing. As soon as possible, the landlord went over.

Mr. Davidson had never reached shore.
His body was found in some drift-wood in a
slough, seven or eight miles below, about
two months afterward. They notified Burrows & Prettyman, at once, of his disap-
pearance and supposed death. His only
brother was in California. His only other
relatives were his mother and a sister, who
lived in Davenport. We at once informed
them, and they said to spare no expense to
find the body, and we wrote up, offering

Railway, which here crosses the Mississippi, was pushed
westward into northern Iowa, McGregor was an important river point at which the produce for 100 miles
or more inland found its way to market.

a reward, and also hired a man to search for him.

As there was no one to attend to Davidson's purchases, I assumed all liabilities, refunding to Henning & Woodruff what had been advanced, and received the produce on my own account, and paid all charges against it.

The first winter after Mr. Prettyman and myself made a dissolution in the produce business, was a very profitable one in porkpacking. I made a large profit on pork, and also had an Indian contract for flour, which made me considerable.

In just six months after I gave Burrows & Prettyman the note for thirty thousand dollars, I had made the money to pay it, and, according to agreement, took it up. I also made for John C. Forey fifteen hundred dollars, on two thousand he had left with me for packing on his account.

Mr. Forey, long since dead, was well known to some of our citizens now living. He was a man of education and refinement, and some means. He took a fancy to Davenport, and expressed a desire to go into business in the town, which I encouraged, and advised him to try the pork business, telling him I had more business than I wished, and if he would go into that business, I would withdraw, and do everything I could to assist him. It was understood, in the spring, that he would come out in the summer or early fall, in time to make arrangements for the season's packing.

With this understanding, having a good offer for my pork-house and lot, as much as I thought them worth, I sold them. I also found a buyer for my lard-kettles, press, tools, etc., and thought I was done packing pork.

Chapter 25

Once More in the Pork-Packing Line.—The Greatest
Packing Season on Record.—Every Warehouse and
Cellar Filled with Frozen Hogs.—Difficulty in Ob-
taining Ready Money.—Financial Troubles Success-
fully Surmounted.—A Profitable Season's Business.

IN the years 1834–54, business was very
much depressed, especially among bankers, on account of the wildcat nature
of our western circulation. It was almost
impossible for the banks to furnish eastern
exchange. Our currency consisted of the
State Bank of Illinois and the free banks of
Indiana, and was from ten to twenty per
cent discount.

When navigation closed, and winter operations were resumed, funds were necessary
to take care of the hog crop, and to receive
the winter accumulation of grain, and not
many operators had the money or credit to
carry on the usual winter operations. I saw,
with regret, that Mr. Forey was not going to
be able to fill his engagement. I wrote to
him repeatedly, informing him of the necessity of his laying in his salt, putting up some
kind of building, and providing the necessary
tools for the work. He at last wrote to me

that it would be impossible for him to do anything that season. He was settling up a large estate in Louisiana, which he had had in charge for two years, and had hoped to close out that summer, but found he could not. I told our farmers I should not pack that season, and they had better hunt some other market. Soon word was received from Muscatine that there was to be no packing done there. As it was necessary that the hog crop should be taken care of, and as there seemed to be no other person to do the business, I was compelled to pack.

I fixed up the lower floor of my Ætna Mill for a pork-house and the boiler-room for a rendering-house. This was the fall previous to the mill breaking down. I succeeded in finding some lard-kettles and pork tools in Muscatine and Rock Island City. I bought most of my salt, of which I needed a large quantity, from the packers in Muscatine, as they had no use for it there, and, about two weeks later than usual, I began to receive hogs. As I had the Muscatine hogs, as well as our own, I packed, that winter, nineteen thousand, which was twice as many as I ever packed before. Muscatine generally packed more than we did.

The hogs were brought in dressed and frozen, and could not be cut more than half as fast as at present. We received them four times as fast as we could cut them, and soon had every warehouse and cellar in town filled with frozen hogs. We worked two sets of hands, night and day.

Our receipts of wheat were also very heavy, and we kept Cook & Sargent's bank about empty. Money was so very tight, everywhere, that winter, that Woodruff insisted upon Cook & Sargent taking half I drew in ninety-day bills. There was no better paper than James E. Woodruff's acceptances in the New York market, and as all banks at the West were in want of eastern exchange, it was no trouble to sell our drafts, if we could find any bank that had the money. We sent three times to Nathan Corwith & Co.'s bank, in Galena, getting ten thousand dollars each time; also to Mr. Mobley, banker, in Dubuque, for all he could spare. We were using from five to ten thousand dollars a day during the pork season.

When at the height of the season, the receipts were so heavy that I tried to keep the hogs from coming to Davenport. A large part of them came from Cedar and Linn counties. The road branched near Red Oak Grove, one branch going to Muscatine and the other to Davenport. Muscatine was the nearer town. I hired a man to stay at the forks of the road and try to turn the farmers to Muscatine or Burlington. I had been using money, for some time, twice as fast as Cook & Sargent could use ninety-day drafts. They told me I could check on, without regard to my account, and when they wanted a draft, they would come and get it. My account was soon over-checked one hundred and twenty thousand dollars, where it stayed for some time.

One day, after banking hours, Ebenezer Cook came over to the pork-house and said:

"Burrows, you have nearly broken us to-day. We are cleaned out. You will have to hold up. We could not pay your checks another day to save our lives."

I told him I could not stop. There was a good deal of stuff still to come in.

He said: "You can buy it, and give your notes, payable in the spring. You are the only man on the river who has been paying cash this winter."

I told him I would think the matter over during the night. In the morning, I filled out a check on Cook & Sargent's bank, "payable the 1st of next April, acceptance waived," and told Cook & Sargent I should use them in payments that day. The next day I should use the same form, only changing the time of payment to the 2d day of April, and so on, day after day, making each one day later, so as to make each day's payment correspond with each day's purchase. The plan worked well. There was no trouble. I told the farmers there was in our store the best stock of goods in town. They could have anything they wanted, at as cheap rates as the goods could be bought in the States. Any one preferring gold, payable in June, instead of currency in April, could have it. Many preferred waiting until June for gold, and I brought sixty thousand dollars from St. Louis, on the 1st of June, and deposited it in Cook & Sargent's bank, to pay those gold checks, some of which were not presented for payment until the following winter.

All our winter operations turned out well, and that winter's business was the heaviest I ever transacted. The store sold a large amount of goods. About the 1st of March, Mr. Prettyman found that he had on hand some six thousand dollars of the paper of the free banks of Indiana, which was quoted at only about eighty cents on the dollar. He sorted it over, putting each bank's paper by itself, and, grip-sack in hand, went from bank to bank, all over Indiana, and presented it for redemption, taking in payment exchange on Cincinnati, Chicago, and St. Louis, or other good current funds. By this means it netted him about ninety-five per cent.

Chapter 26

Western Flour Popular Far from Home.—From the Shores of the Mississippi to the Banks of the Hudson. —How They Liked Davenport's Flour in the East.— One Brand at a Premium.—Cost of Shipping.

MY pork had been bought very low, and the falling off in the amount of packing through the West, that season, caused a material advance in pork products the ensuing spring.

Our Albion Mills brand of flour had become so well established, and in such demand, that it was a pleasure to manufacture it. I could not half supply the demand.

About the middle of June, wishing to make some repairs on the mill before harvest, which would require about a month, I concluded, while this was being done, that, as I had plenty of money, I would spend the time at my old home in New Jersey, where I was born and bred, and have a good time.

My wife and myself took a boat to Steubenville, Ohio, where my daughter was attending school, at the female seminary; and, taking her with us, we went to Albany, New York, by rail, where we arrived in the morning. My daughter wanted me to go to New York by boat, so that she could see the scenery on the Hudson River. I consented to do so.

As the boat was not to start until afternoon, I took a walk over Albany. Passing along Water Street, where the heavy business seemed to be done, I cast my eye into a large warehouse or store, and saw the lower floor half filled with flour branded "Albion Mills, Davenport, Iowa." On walking in, I saw two gentlemen standing near the door. I passed them, and stood looking at the flour. One of the gentlemen walked up to me and said:

"Do you wish to buy some flour?"

I said: "No, sir. I came in out of curiosity. I live in the town where that flour is manufactured. I am surprised to see it here, and have a curiosity to know how it came to be here."

He replied: "I bought this lot of five hundred barrels in New York City." He added: "Do you know the man who makes this flour?"

I answered: "Yes; very well. I am the man."

He said: "You are the very man I want to see. I want you to supply me with that flour. It is the best I ever handled. I never sold it to a baker, that he did not want more. It is the strongest flour I ever saw. One-half the men dealing in flour don't know anything about it; but I was a baker before I went into the flour trade, and know from experience what is wanted."

He said he had written to Chicago a number of times, trying to buy some more of the flour, but could find none in that market. He wanted to get it direct, as buying in New York cost him ten cents a barrel to get it back to Albany, which town it had just passed through.

He said: "Some of the Moline flour, made by D. B. Sears, is as good as yours; but it is not of uniform grade. Your flour runs even, and we never have any complaint."

I told him I had an arrangement with my commission house, Woodruff & Co., of New York, that no Albion flour should be offered for sale East, except through them, and that was the reason he could not find it in Chicago; but he could get Woodruff & Co., of New York to stop it in transit at Albany, and so save the freight back. I mentioned the circumstance to Woodruff the next day. He said he would write to the house in Albany, and arrange to have whatever flour they wanted stopped there. Woodruff said the arrangement we had made with them worked well. Our flour was all engaged before it reached them. They never went out of their office to sell it; any one wanting it had to come to them.

"And," he said, "it is fifty cents a barrel more to you if the buyer seeks us than it would be if we sought him. It is a pleasure to handle your flour, and Fagin's, of St. Louis. Fagin's brand is in the same demand as yours."

Chapter 27

More About the Banking Business in Davenport.—
Trouble Over Wildcat Currency.—Cook & Sargent's Florence Notes.—Burrows & Prettyman
Try Their Luck.—All Goes Well.

AFTER passing a few weeks among the
scenes of my childhood, I returned
West to my business. As I have
said, business was very much depressed by
the state of our currency. People had lost
confidence in the State banks of Illinois and
the free banks of Indiana. Small change had
about disappeared, and, instead, many persons gave their own individual tickets,
printed on pasteboard or fine paper, as the
case might be, payable when presented in
amounts equal to one dollar.

For some time, Cook & Sargent, besides
circulating Clark & Brother's acceptances,
had been paying out their own issue of the
Bank of Florence, Nebraska. Nebraska
at that time was almost a wilderness. The
money was redeemable at Florence.[29] Cook

[29] Here is a good illustration of the methods which
characterized the operations of the wildcat banks. Save
for the migration westward over the Oregon and
Mormon Trails, which traversed northern Nebraska

& Sargent had depended on me to pay out their circulation, which I had been doing for some time.

I found this state of things likely to continue indefinitely, and, believing that Burrows & Prettyman's credit was as good as Cook & Sargent's, especially among the farmers, we thought if that kind of circulation was profitable, we might as well circulate our own paper as that of others.

Mr. Prettyman and myself talked the matter over, and decided that we would enter into the business, and issue one hundred thousand dollars. We sent to Rawdon, Wright, Hatch & Edson, New York City, the firm which printed all bank bills at that time, and ordered what we wanted. They informed us, in reply, that they were not in the habit of engraving and printing such matter, except for banks, and requested us to send them references as to the standing of our house.

from east to west, prior to 1854 that region was practically a complete wilderness. Florence, a present-day suburb of Omaha, was the eastern terminus of the Mormon Trail, established in 1845–46. By locating their bank at this distant and obscure point, and circulating their banknotes at Davenport, the firm of Cook and Sargent sought to render it difficult or impossible for holders of the notes to present them for redemption.

We referred them to James E. Woodruff & Co., of New York. They then filled our order. They threw in ten thousand dollars, sending us one hundred and ten thousand, for which they charged us eight hundred dollars, the price agreed upon for one hundred thousand. They were beautifully engraved, printed on the nicest kind of bank-note paper, and looked as well as any bank bills in circulation.

I called on Cook & Sargent, and told them what we proposed to do, and asked them what they thought about it. Ebenezer Cook rather threw cold water on the project at first, but Sargent and John P. Cook seemed to be in favor of it. I told them we should do it anyhow, and I hoped, when they thought the matter over, that we could arrange with them to make our checks bankable. We would still continue to pay out Florence, giving the farmers whichever they preferred, and we also would let Cook & Sargent have all our eastern exchange, as we made it, from day to day, and which they, at that time, could not have run their bank six months without. In return, they agreed to protect Burrows & Prettyman's circulation, treating it the same as they did their own.

In a short time we began to pay out our checks. They went just as well as Florence.

Cook & Sargent took them the same as
Florence. The railroad took them, also the
steamboats, and we had no trouble to circulate them. We calculated the profit on the
circulation at ten thousand dollars a year,
which was for the benefit of the firm of Burrows & Prettyman, instead of J. M. D.
Burrows.[30]

[30] These notes, it will be seen, had nothing back of
them save the faith and credit of Burrows and Prettyman. The yearly profit of $10,000 is evidently calcu-
lated at 10% interest on the quantity of notes issued.
A widely-known example of the same kind of operation
as the one here described was the notes issued by
George Smith of early Chicago and Milwaukee financial
fame. He founded the Chicago Marine and Fire
Insurance Company in 1836 and the Wisconsin Marine
and Fire Insurance Company in 1839, and for twenty
years, until driven from circulation by the spread of the
free-banking system in the fifties, "George Smith's
money" circulated far and wide at par, bringing enormous profits to the issuing firm.

Chapter 28

My First and Only Experience as a Steamboat Captain.
—A Late Trip Down River with the Staunch Little
Mary C.—We Make a Safe Run and Lots of Money
Out of It.—Incidents Going and Coming.

IN the summer and fall of 1856 or 1857, we were handling large amounts of St. Louis freight, and made an arrangement with Captain John Coleman to run his boat, the *Mary C.*, which was a good low-water craft, of light draught and fair tonnage, from Davenport to St. Louis for us, on condition that we give him all the freight he could carry during the season.

We kept the *Mary C.* running all the fall. When navigation was about to close, we informed Captain Coleman, as he was leaving on the trip before the last, that it would not be safe to make more than another trip. We had a large amount of freight in Camanche, and it was understood that when the boat returned from this trip she was to go up with one barge and get it, and leave another barge at Davenport, which we were to load while the steamer was gone.

When the *Mary C.* returned from St. Louis, the weather had turned much colder, and Captain Coleman wanted to run down to Rockingham Slough and lay up. He had been detained at the Lower Rapids three or four days, and it was very uncertain whether another trip could be made. All the other boats had withdrawn for the season. With great reluctance, Captain Coleman at last started off for Camanche. During his absence we loaded the other barge and had it all ready to pull out, so as to cause only a few hours delay when the steamer arrived, on her way to St. Louis.

On her down trip from Camanche, the *Mary C.* was detained two days at Le Claire, on account of high winds, and when she arrived at Davenport it was snowing and freezing, and Captain Coleman was discouraged. He said it would be impossible to make the trip. After a great deal of talk and expostulation, he said:

"I'm sick, and unable to go. If you see fit to take the boat yourself, and go with her, you can do so."

I asked him what he would charge me for the use of his boat.

He said: "Nothing at all. All I require is that you shall return her this fall, if possible, in as good order as she is now; but if you are frozen up, she is to be taken care of at your expense, and delivered at Davenport in the spring."

I told Captain Coleman I would not take his boat without giving him some compensation. I should not attempt to go below Montrose, and would pay him two hundred and fifty dollars for the trip. I made immediate arrangements to get off. The engineer informed me that the long copper steampipe was unsafe, and would have to be taken off and repaired. This took twenty-four hours precious time.

At last we got off, "Captain" J. M. D. Burrows on deck, Edward Davidson and William Dalzell in the office, and Peter Hall in the pilot-house.

Mr. Hall was then considered as good a pilot as there was on the river. He is the same "Pete" Hall who has been living in a skiff for a number of years, hunting all through the South for ancient relics for the Academy of Sciences of Davenport, and has come to be known as "The Old Man of the Skiff."

We made no landing for anything but wood. It was very cold, and ice was forming rapidly. We did not want any freight, but sped on our way as fast as possible.

Just below New Boston, one of our barges struck a snag and sank. We examined it and found it would have to be abandoned. We went ashore, and entered protest to protect our insurance, and, leaving two men in charge of the barge, we pushed on to Montrose.

On our arrival, I found there were two or three boats at Keokuk, waiting for freight for St. Louis. They had been unable to get over the Rapids, and, having sent their freight in lighters to Montrose, were ready to return to St. Louis. I sent the first clerk down to attend to reshipping, and secured lighters immediately to lighten over. As soon as we could discharge our cargo, we ran back to the sunken barge, unloaded her, and returned to Montrose with the load.

The freight from the St. Louis boats had been on the levee at Montrose about a week, well covered with tarpaulins, and the officers did not know what to do with it. As we were going to return empty, they urged us to take it off their hands. It had been shipped at one dollar a hundred pounds from St. Louis to any point between Montrose and Davenport. We offered to receive all the goods we could carry, and deliver them to the owners living between the Rapids, at a dollar a hundred pounds, and a dollar and a quarter a hundred to any point above the Upper Rapids and below Dubuque, these latter goods to be delivered in the spring. After a good deal of dickering, they agreed to our terms, which left them nothing for bringing the goods from St. Louis to Montrose.

While we were loading up, I had the carpenter build an ice-crib at the bow of the *Mary C.*, and kept the pilot watching the amount of water she drew as the loading progressed, telling him to take every pound he thought she could carry safely, and no more. Besides our freight, we got nearly one hundred emigrant passengers, at ten dollars each, to points between the Rapids. We had a tedious trip, having to contend with a river filled with ice, but we succeeded in fighting our way through.

When we arrived at Davenport, as our trip had been so successful, I told the clerk to pay Captain Coleman five hundred dollars, instead of two hundred and fifty dollars, as promised, and to make out a balance-sheet, which he did, and paid over to me three thousand five hundred and fifty dollars, net profit from the up trip. Besides this, my own freight on the down trip, which had gone on to St. Louis, amounted to fully a thousand dollars more, making the profit on the week's steamboating four thousand five hundred and fifty dollars.

Chapter 29

The Beginning of Financial Complications That Led to
a Serious Crisis.—Cook & Sargent's Efforts to Save
Themselves from Disaster.—Calling in Their Florence Currency.—How They Were Accommodated by
Burrows & Prettyman and Other Friends.—Attacks
from Macklot & Corbin and the Press.

IN the latter part of 1858, and in 1859, the
banking house of Macklot & Corbin, of
Davenport, made war on Cook & Sargent's bank, on account of their Wildcat
money. The Davenport *Democrat* also made
almost daily attacks on their circulation, and
the merchants, too, became dissatisfied, and
said this state of things was an injury; that
it kept out eastern money, and made exchange too high. Between Corbin and the
Democrat, it became so hot for Cook &
Sargent that they saw they would be compelled to withdraw their Florence money.
To enable them to do this, they procured
accommodation paper of Antoine Le Claire,
George L. Davenport, Davenport & Rogers,
of Le Claire, Burrows & Prettyman, and
J. M. D. Burrows—from any one, in short,
who was esteemed good in bank circles at
the East.

George B. Sargent, one of the firm, went East, and established a branch of the firm in Boston, for the purpose of negotiating this accommodation paper, and attending to other kiting. As the money was realized on this paper, it was used for redeeming Florence. Had it not been for this assistance, they could not have retired their circulation, and their failure would have occurred at a much earlier date than it did.

In looking over my papers for that winter (1858–59), just before their failure, I find receipts from Cook & Sargent for six bills of exchange drawn by J. M. D. Burrows on Burrows & Prettyman, and accepted by them, payable at the Bank of North America, New York, and the Bank of Massachusetts, Boston, at sixty days. These bills of exchange were for forty thousand dollars. They were acknowledged, in the receipts, as accommodation paper for the benefit of Cook & Sargent, and were to be protected by them when due. The amount of such accommodation paper was generally over a hundred thousand dollars. When it matured, they got new bills to take its place.

This state of things continued until Cook & Sargent's failure, an account of which will be given hereafter. This assistance of borrowed paper put Cook & Sargent in possession of funds to redeem their circulation, but Macklot & Corbin's course in refusing to recognize the wildcat currency, together with the severe strictures of the *Democrat*, compelled them to withdraw their circulation faster than was convenient.

When we issued Burrows & Prettyman's money, it was understood that we would redeem it in Florence, which was always bankable at Cook & Sargent's bank, and they did more business than all the other banks put together.

Austin Corbin[31] was a very shrewd, cautious man. Since that day of small things, he has made his mark in the financial world. As everybody knows, he has become one of the great railroad magnates of the East. I have every reason to speak well of him. He always treated me with courtesy, and I never heard of his trying to injure Burrows & Prettyman's circulation, except as it was connected with Cook & Sargent, when they were at war with each other.

[31] For the career of Austin Corbin see *Dict. Am. Biog.* He was a man of great financial ability, whose ideas were frequently far in advance of his age. He conceived and executed the project of developing Coney Island as a resort for New York City's teeming millions. He labored to develop a rapid transit subway system for New York a generation before the community was ready to pay serious attention to such a project.

If a man wanted to use one hundred dollars in Davenport, or on the river or railroad, or within a circuit of one hundred miles of Davenport, Burrows & Prettyman or Florence would answer his purpose. If he wanted to use it in traveling East, it would not answer.

A man would bring in a hundred dollars of our checks, saying he wanted something he could use abroad. We would tell him we had nothing but Florence, which was bankable at Cook & Sargent's. We would then count him out one hundred dollars in Florence, which he would take to Cook & Sargent's bank, and get in exchange one hundred dollars of Burrows & Prettyman's checks— and the man was just where he had been fifteen minutes before. This was called, in those days, swapping cats. We saw this could not continue, and were retiring our circulation as fast as we could, but the necessity came upon us in bad times. Crops in 1858 and 1859 were almost a failure. Farmers could not pay. Burrows & Prettyman had, on the first day of January, 1859, one hundred and sixty-five thousand dollars outstanding on their books and notes, and I do not believe they ever collected more than twenty-five thousand dollars of that amount.

Chapter 30

ONE morning when I visited the bank, Ebenezer Cook called me into the bank parlor, and said:

"We are getting in our Florence very fast. We now have about forty thousand dollars outstanding, and must get it in. Your circulation hampers us. How do you think it would work if we received your money on special deposit only?"

I answered: "It would ruin us. Any change from the present state of things would be bad for both of us. The best thing we can do is to retire our currency as fast as possible."

He opened the door and called in John P. Cook, and said: "John, Burrows says that change will ruin him."

John P. Cook replied: "No, it will not. His credit with the farmers is so good it won't hurt him at all. Burrows, we will do all we can to help you. We will explain to our depositors that we believe you are as good as ever; that we will take your currency for any notes or any indebtedness to us."

I told the Messrs. Cook that they were not standing up to their agreement. As to hampering them, I could not see it. I said: "You have made thousands of dollars out of what eastern exchange I have given you. I let you have it at par. You sold it at from ten to twenty per cent premium, and exacted of me a promise that I would not let our merchants have any, but let you have all, for which favors you agreed to treat our circulation the same as your own. And then, again, you have our accommodation paper, which you are using to retire Florence."

When I left them they were undecided, and made no move until about three o'clock, when they began to enter our checks as special deposits. Two or three merchants, favorable to me, came to the store just after the bank closed, showed me their bank books, and asked an explanation. I told them what had occurred, and they were very indignant at the manner in which Cook & Sargent had treated us.

That afternoon there was a good deal of excitement, especially in the lower end of town, and I knew there would be a big run on us in the morning. I went home heartsick. I could neither eat nor sleep. Long before daylight I drank two cups of strong coffee, and went up town to see Ebenezer Cook. He lived at that time at the corner of Third and Brady streets, on the lot where Durfee's jewelry establishment now stands. It was very early—an hour before day. I pounded on his door. He put his head out of the window to see who it was. I told him I wanted to see him, and he came down and let me in. We had a long talk. I think he regretted the step they had taken, but he said it was too late now. He did not think it would injure us as much as I anticipated.

Seeing nothing could be done, I went down to the mill, and stayed there until nine o'clock, when I went over to face the music. I found at least a hundred persons at the store. They had their hands full of currency. I spoke pleasantly to them.

I said: "Gentlemen, you come too many at a time. If there were but a few of you, I might do something for you. Your checks are just as good now as they were three months ago. Anything in this store or the mill you can have in exchange for our checks, as cheaply as if you paid in gold. There are in the back yard one thousand barrels of Kanawha salt, which we received only a few days ago. You can have all you

want of it at the lowest wholesale cash price
—the cheapest in town; and we shall continue to take the checks, in store and mill,
until the last one is redeemed. If you are
owing anything at Cook & Sargent's bank,
they will take them from you."

Some one spoke up, and said: "That is
honest. You need not be scared."

At this, about half of them went away.
The rest went to trading.

As regards Burrows & Prettyman's circulation, I am glad to have an opportunity to
say that we continued to redeem it until the
last check was presented, and never paid
less than the face called for. I have five or
six of those checks laid away as keepsakes,
and they are the only ones I know of in
existence.

Chapter 31

ONE morning when I was in the bank,
John P. Cook picked up a large
business envelope, and said to me:

"Burrows, here is a package of your circulation, one hundred dollars. We received it
from a Pittsburgh bank this morning. I
don't know how it got there; probably they
got it from some traveler. They told us
to do the best we could with it, and remit."
He added: "They don't know the value
of it. Give me fifty dollars, and you can
have it."

I said: "No, Mr. Cook, I will not do it. I
have never paid less than the face of those
checks, and I have got too near through to
begin scalping now."

I was drawing some money. I threw down
one hundred dollars, and took the package.
Whether the Pittsburgh bank got fifty or one
hundred dollars, I do not know.

If there is anything I pride myself upon in
my business career, it is the Burrows &

Prettyman check business. The checks were issued at a time when the business of the city and the situation of the county needed them, and they helped to keep the wheels of commerce moving. A month never passes, even now, but some one speaks to me about those checks, and how they helped business. We never had more than a hundred and ten thousand dollars out; while I think Cook & Sargent had out three hundred thousand dollars of Florence. I know of their burning two hundred thousand dollars of Florence at one time; at least, they said they did, and there was still a great deal in circulation.

Cook & Sargent receiving our checks on special deposit only, injured our paper at the East, which reacted on them. They had generally one hundred thousand dollars of Burrows & Prettyman's and J. M. D. Burrows' drafts and acceptances—accommodation paper, which they depended on to keep themselves afloat; and George B. Sargent found, after this, it was not so easy to dispose of them, and the bank was in a critical condition.

About this time, Ebenezer Cook came to me and said they were very much in need of money; that he had been to see if Le Claire would indorse my note for twenty thousand dollars. Le Claire had promised to do so if I would give him a mortgage on my beautiful home, Clifton.

I said: "I cannot do that, Mr. Cook; that is my home."

The next day Ebenezer Cook called again. We had about the same talk, with the same result. He called again the third day, and was very urgent. He said if they did not get immediate help, they would have to suspend. They had received a telegram from Sargent that day, saying he could realize the money on my note, and wanted it forthwith.

Ebenezer Cook said: "Burrows, if you will do it, if the worst ever comes to the worst, I will take care of you."

The worst did come to the worst, soon, and he did not take care of me. He never raised a finger.

I gave the note, Le Claire indorsed it, and had to pay the twenty thousand dollars, and his estate took my place.

I never would have given way, had I not known that if Cook & Sargent suspended, they would carry Burrows & Prettyman with them. We, with others, were on their paper for enough to break us all.

Chapter 32

Events Preliminary to the Cook & Sargent Collapse.—
My Milling Operations in 1852-53.—Breaking Out of
the Crimean War.—A Great Boom in American
Wheat.—My Preparations to Meet It.—Opening of
the Chicago & Rock Island Railroad.

IN relating the foregoing facts, I have
anticipated somewhat the chronological
order of events, and I now find it necessary to retrograde a few years, that the
reader may have a consecutive story of the
developments which were climaxed in the
failure of Cook & Sargent, with the attendant disastrous effects upon Burrows &
Prettyman and others.

In 1852-53, as I had been very successful
and had made a good deal of money, I
decided to double the capacity of my flouring
mill. At the same time, I tore down the Ætna
Mill, and put up Burrows' Block, on the levee,
and also built Clifton, my home already referred to. I spent, in these three improvements,
one hundred and sixty thousand dollars, and
used more than two millions of brick, all I
could get in Davenport and Rock Island.

About this time the Crimean War was
declared. In the spring of 1854, I sent my

wife East, promising to join her there in the
latter part of May. But we had, that summer, a great flood. I could not run my mill
for about two months. Burrows & Prettyman's store was in the water, which was
nearly two feet deep on the first floor. We
had to put in a false floor, and also to run a
boat from the corner of Front and Brady
streets to our store, to ferry our customers.

I could not leave while this state of things
lasted, and did not get away until late in
June.

I had been watching the markets and the
foreign news. Most persons thought the war
would all end in smoke, as it has ended many
times since; but I believed Russia would fight.
Others thought the war would not affect our
markets; but I thought it would, as Russia
exported a large quantity of wheat, especially from the port of Sevastopol, and when
that port was blockaded, I believed there
would be a sharp advance in breadstuffs.

I was in New York during the early part
of July, and visited my old friend, James E.
Woodruff, at Woodruff & Co.'s office, in
Broad Street. I had many talks with Mr.
Woodruff about the prospect of the business
season about to open. Breadstuff markets
were very much depressed, both in the East
and the West.

Woodruff asked me what I was going to pay for wheat. I told him fifty cents a bushel.

He said: "I don't know what you are going to do with it at that price. There is not a market in the world that you can ship wheat to where it will net you more than forty cents a bushel. You ought not to pay to exceed forty cents." He added: "You are too good to the farmers. You pay too much for produce. You always pay higher prices than any of our customers. You work harder, for less money, than any man I ever knew."

"Well," said I, "we are going to have a heavy crop of wheat, and I have doubled the capacity of my mill. Our farmers will not sell wheat freely at less than fifty cents a bushel. Burrows & Prettyman have a large amount standing out which they must get in, and it will require fifty cents a bushel to make collections. I have more faith in the future than you have. I intend to ship everything to New York—all my flour and surplus wheat, and don't care how long it is on the way; the longer the better, because I am satisfied the prices are going to be much higher."

I returned home. On my way, I stopped one day in Chicago, to see how the markets were. Flint & Wheeler were the strongest and heaviest grain men in Chicago then, and had the largest elevator in the city. They took me on 'Change, and showed me various samples of new winter wheat, which was just beginning to come in from Southern Illinois, and selling, that day, at sixty cents a bushel. I had a long talk with them about the fall business. They coincided with Woodruff that forty cents was a generous price, and all I ought to pay.

Our railroad, the Chicago & Rock Island, had just been opened, and freight was very high, being about twenty cents a bushel for wheat from Davenport to Chicago, and then an added expense of about two cents a bushel for receiving, selling, etc.

Fifty cents a bushel for spring wheat in Davenport, with freight and expenses twenty-two cents in Chicago, making the price seventy-two cents a bushel, when the best of fall wheat was selling at sixty cents, did look somewhat venturesome; but, in my whole experience, I never felt so sure of a season's business as I did then. My friends thought I would ruin myself. I went contrary to the advice of James E. Woodruff and Flint & Wheeler, whose judgment I generally considered superior to my own.

Chapter 33

An Unparalleled Wheat Crop in Iowa.—Buying It All
In at Seemingly Exorbitant Prices.—Luck Favors the
Speculator.—The Investing of Sevastopol Causes
Enormous Profits.—$100,000 in Sixty Days.—Even
Disaster Makes Money for Me.—Beginning of the
End.

I ARRIVED home from my eastern trip
about nine o'clock in the morning. After
looking over the store and mill, I went
home, and, taking an early dinner, immediately drove into the country to examine
the crops.

Such a crop of wheat Scott County never
produced before nor since. Farmers were
beginning to harvest. Our land was new,
and in condition to produce its very best.
Club wheat had recently been introduced,
and nearly all the growing crop was of that
variety. It stood thick and even on the
ground, nearly five feet high, and well
headed. For six inches below the head, the
straw was as yellow as gold.

Wheat ran, that year, from thirty to forty
bushels to the acre. What was very remarkable, the quality of the wheat was all alike,
all graded No. 1. You could not get an

inferior quality, even if you paid a premium for it. This extraordinary crop of wheat made me still more sanguine, and I felt in my very bones that this was the time to pitch in.

The heaviest dealers in produce in Davenport, besides myself, were Graham & Kepner. I told them I was going to control the wheat market of Davenport that fall, and that I should keep the price of wheat about two cents above prices in Muscatine, which, at that time, was our only competitor. I also told them that I intended to draw the wheat from Cedar and Linn counties away from Muscatine.

I made this proposition to them: "I will give you five cents a bushel for all the wheat you will buy between now and the first of next December. You shall put it in my mill, on the railroad cars, or on a steamboat, or wherever I shall instruct you. I will give you the price each morning which you are to pay that day. You shall pay just what I pay. I will never bid against you. You will furnish your own money. I want your bills of lading and vouchers every Saturday, and you are to bring in your bill every Monday morning, and I will pay you."

In those days I drew on my shipments only once a week.

Graham & Kepner accepted my proposition. I used to pay them from ten to twenty thousand dollars every Monday morning. They made an arrangement with a Mr. Campbell, a banker on Main Street, to furnish the money. This Mr. Campbell, by the way, committed suicide in the bank, a year or so afterward, by shooting himself.

Mr. Graham has told me since, repeatedly, that they never did as well any season as they did under this arrangement with me. At the commencement, I paid ten cents a bushel more than anyone else dared to pay.

I had all Graham & Kepner's wheat put into cars for shipment to New York, as I received from farmers all I could grind. Graham & Kepner arranged with the railroad company to place cars where the farmers could get at them and unload their wheat into the car, thus saving a second handling and the additional expense.

As soon as I had made my arrangement with Graham & Kepner, I went over to Chicago to make arrangements with Flint & Wheeler to receive and forward my shipment. I told them I expected to be able to load a vessel once a week, and that I did not want my wheat inspected. All I wanted was to have them receive the flour and wheat, from day to day, as it arrived, and hold it until they had enough to load a vessel, when they were to consign to Woodruff & Co., New York.

It took but a short time to show that I was in luck. Sevastopol was invested. Bread-stuffs advanced in Europe. Russia's ports were blockaded. Her grain was locked up. The first of my fifty-cent wheat brought two dollars and twenty-five cents a bushel in New York. I made more than one hundred thousand dollars between the first of August and the first of December. Most of the money was made the first sixty days, when wheat was low. I began buying at fifty cents, and in October was paying a dollar and forty cents a bushel. At the latter price only ordinary profits were made. Everything seemed to favor me that fall. One propellor, loaded entirely with my wheat and flour, exploded on the lake, and sunk, the cargo being a total loss, and I made four thousand dollars by it. It was insured in New York City, and I saved the freight from Davenport to New York.

From the first of December of that year (1854) until some time in March, 1856, during the Crimean War, I did a fairly good business.

Chapter 34

A Sudden Taste of Adversity.—Death of Nicholas, Czar of Russia, and Slump in the Wheat Market.—A Loss of $200,000 in a Single Day.—Distress Among Dealers All Along the Mississippi.—Small Disasters Follow the Big One.—The Camanche Cyclone with the Rest.

THEN came a dreadful blow. First, the news of the taking of Sevastopol; then, in a short time, the death of Nicholas, Czar of Russia. At the news of his death, everyone knew the war was at an end, and prices of produce fell instantly all over the United States—wheat from fifty to sixty cents a bushel; flour, three dollars a barrel, and everything else in proportion; and the decline continued day after day. I went to bed, on the night the news arrived, two hundred thousand dollars poorer than I had arisen the same morning.

I had on the market, and unsold, six thousand barrels of flour, and, in Davenport, one hundred and fifty thousand bushels of wheat, and all my winter's packing, not a dollar's worth of which had been sold.

That drop in prices was an overwhelming catastrophe. It broke up nearly every dealer on the Mississippi River, and was really what finally broke Burrows & Prettyman. We worked along a number of years, badly crippled. This revulsion in the market brought on stagnation and hard times, and there was not much opportunity for a man to retrieve his fortunes.

I had made a good deal of money, but had laid it out in building, and in some outside speculations, which entailed heavy losses.

The opening of the Chicago & Rock Island Railroad rather bewildered me. It revolutionized the mode of doing business. Heretofore, a few men at each business point had done the bulk of the business required, and a great deal of money and good credit were necessary. We always had been compelled to hold our accumulation from November to April, and not many had either the nerve or the means to do it.

When the railroad got into operation, produce men were as thick as potato-bugs. If a man could raise two hundred and fifty dollars, he could begin business. That amount would buy a car-load of wheat. In the morning he would engage a car, have it put where he could load it, and have the farmer put his wheat, barley, or oats, as the case might be, in the car. By three o'clock in the afternoon the car would be loaded and shipped.

In the pork season it was the same way. As I have said before, the hogs in those days were brought in ready dressed. A produce dealer would place a scale on the sidewalk in some convenient place, weigh his hogs as he bought them, pile them up on the sidewalk, and, in the afternoon, load them up and ship them. Dealers were at no expense of rent or labor.

One of my outside speculations referred to already, was the building of a warehouse at the freight depot, which we thought would be necessary. We bought the lot just west of where the Crescent Mill now stands, and paid four thousand dollars cash for it. After keeping it several years, and finding we did not need it, we sold it for two thousand dollars.

I got the idea that it would be necessary, in order to retain our trade, to follow the railroad. We were induced to start a branch store in Fulton; also, a manufactory for reaping-machines and seed-sowers in the same place; also, to invest in the Fulton steam flouring-mill and operate it. And then, still worse, to start another branch store in Iowa City, where a fast young man soon sunk twenty thousand dollars for us. The firm was Burrows, Prettyman & Babcock, and the fast young man's name was Babcock.

In a trade I made with George L. Davenport, he conveyed to me a one-third interest in the only steam saw-mill in Camanche, which investment was also an unfortunate operation. The only thing expected of me seemed to be to furnish money to buy logs. I don't think I ever received a dollar in return from the concern. If I did, I have no recollection of it.

Then came the great cyclone which swept over Camanche, almost destroying the town, and killing many of its inhabitants. The cyclone blew away and destroyed our lumber, and badly damaged the mill.

In these various outside speculations, I lost not less than one hundred thousand dollars, which reflected no credit upon my business sagacity.

Chapter 35

Cook & Sargent in a Strait.—Those Florence Notes
Cause the Trouble.—History of the Currency Riot of
1859.—Ebenezer Cook's House Smashed.—The Rioters Visit Clifton, but Think Better of Their Purpose.
—An Exciting Epoch.

THESE great losses made hard times
for me. We were retiring our circulation as fast as we could. As I have
said before, the necessity came upon us at a
bad time. For two years our crops were a
failure, our farmers were unable to meet
their engagements, and I do not think I ever
experienced a worse time than in 1859.

Cook & Sargent, spurred on by Austin
Corbin and the *Democrat*, were still taking in
Florence as fast as they could, but there was
much grumbling and dissatisfaction.

Ebenezer Cook was Mayor that year. One
evening in the summer of 1859, some one
came to my house and informed me that I
had better go up town; that he understood
there was likely to be a currency riot that
night. After supper, I went up town and
held a consultation with Mr. Prettyman.
We had iron shutters on the store. I advised
him to close the shutters and stay inside,

while I stayed outside. An hour later, a mob came from the east, along Front Street.

They passed along Front Street, between the store and the mill, in perfect silence, without halting or making a demonstration, turned the corner of Perry Street, and marched up. I surmised where they were going, and, getting ahead of them, went to Ebenezer Cook's house and told him what was on hand.

In a few minutes the crowd came. They did not lose much time, but began to hoot, and to pelt, with rocks and clubs, Mr. Cook's beautiful new house, into which he had just moved. The crowd soon smashed in the front windows. Mr. Cook's family and I were in the front part of the house, but had to go to the kitchen for safety.

After pretty effectually smashing in the front windows, the crowd began to withdraw. Mr. Cook was very much excited. Being Mayor of the town, he thought this attack not only an outrage on his rights as a citizen, but an indignity to his official station. He said if he had known it in time, he would have had a cannon there.

As the mob left, some one cried out, "Now for Burrows!" Another voice said, "Let Burrows alone;" but about one-third of the rioters started toward my house, nearly a mile and a half distant, the rest scattering to their homes.

I had a horse near the mill. Leaping upon him, I started for home, where I arrived much sooner than the mob did. After telling my wife what was going on, and not to be alarmed, that no one would hurt her, I closed all the shutters, and went outside. I told my wife I should not go away, but would remain in the yard. I took with me a double-barrel gun which I always kept loaded and handy.

Taking a position east of my house, at the forks of the road, in the shrubbery on my own premises, where no one could see me, I waited for some time. Finally, along came the mob. They halted before they reached the forks of the road, and held a council of war. I could hear their voices, but could not make out what they said.

After considerable noisy debate, some one cried out loudly, "Let Burrows alone!" Some-one else said, "Let Burrows alone!" and the whole crowd left.

And that was the end of the currency riot of 1859.

Chapter 36

The Storm Thickens Over Cook & Sargent.—A Note
Protested by Macklot & Corbin.—No Funds in the
Rival Bank.—Unsuccessful Efforts to Stay the Im-
pending Catastrophe.—A Day of Anxiety.

ON the 15th day of December, 1859,
the afternoon before the failure of
Cook & Sargent, about fifteen minutes after three o'clock, Mr. Prettyman came
over to the mill, and said:

"I forgot to inform you, this morning, that
we have a note to pay to-day, at Macklot &
Corbin's bank."

I asked: "How much is it?"

He said: "Three hundred and some twenty-
odd dollars."

I said: "I will go and see about it;" and I
started for Cook & Sargent's bank.

On my way, I stopped at Macklot &
Corbin's, and told them the note had been
overlooked, and asked if they would be
satisfied if I paid the note in the morning
when I drew on my shipments. They said
the note would have to be protested to protect themselves.

I returned to the store and told our book-
keeper to hand me a package of city and

county orders, amounting to eight hundred and twenty dollars, that were in the safe. I then went to Cook & Sargent's bank, told Ebenezer Cook about the note, and that I wanted the money to take it up, and that I would provide for it when I drew on New York, the next morning. He said they had just sent all their bankable funds to the express office, to go to Chicago, and he did not believe they had in the bank that much money such as Corbin would take, holding nothing but Florence and Burrows & Prettyman's money.

He said: "Pay it in the morning. It won't hurt you to have the note lay over."

I said: "You are mistaken. It will hurt us a great deal, for this is some of our new paper."

He replied: "That is so. If it is some of your new paper, you ought to take it up."

Some time before this, our creditors, wishing us to keep along as usual with them, said that if we would meet our new paper as it fell due, they would let the old indebtedness stand, and we could pay it from time to time, as we were able.

Ebenezer Cook called in John P. Cook, and told him what I wanted, explaining that the note was some of our new paper, and ought not to go to protest.

John P. Cook answered: "We have not that much money in bankable funds, or what Macklot & Corbin call bankable funds." He said to me: "Why don't you make your notes payable at our bank? Then we could hold them over for you."

The note was payable at Cook & Sargent's, but was sent to Macklot & Corbin for collection.

John P. Cook added: "Let them protest it if they want to. You take it up to-morrow, and then telegraph that it was overlooked, but that you took it up to-day." As I could do nothing else, I followed his advice.

I returned to the store, and then remembered that I had left my package of county orders on the table in Cook & Sargent's bank parlor. As I expected to go to the bank as soon as it was open in the morning, I did not take the time then to go after the orders.

Chapter 37

The Blow Falls at Last.—Closed at Cook & Sar-
gent's.—A Mob of Angry Depositors.—Desperate
Scene in the Bank.—Ebenezer Cook's Frenzied
Despair.—The Missing Bundle of County Orders.—
Unwarranted Use of Them by the Ruined Bankers.—
A Forgotten Promise.

ON the morning of the 16th of December, 1859, the first place I visited
after coming into town was the mill,
where I spent about an hour examining
what had been done during the night, and
counting the amount of flour on hand, to see
how much money I would have for the day's
business. At a quarter past nine o'clock, I
left the mill to go over to the store to draw
my drafts, preparatory to my visit to the
bank.

In the middle of Front Street I met Cephas
Sanders, one of our clerks, coming over to
see me.

He said: "Mr. Burrows, Cook & Sargent
are not open this morning."

I did not take in the situation at first, and
said: "What is the matter? Is any one
dead?"

He replied: "No, they have busted up."

I said: "I don't believe it."

He answered: "I do. I am going over to see."

It was a pretty cold day. I went over to the store to get my overcoat, and then went straight to the bank. Main Street and Second Street were crowded with townsfolk. It looked as if there was a fire. I should think there were more than one thousand excited persons, many of whom were clamoring for admittance to the bank. There were two policemen guarding the front door. I went to the side door. A policeman was on guard. I told him I wanted to go in. He said he had instructions not to admit any one. I told him it was necessary that I should go in, and that it would be all right.

The policeman stepped aside, and I entered. There was no one in the bank, except the clerks. Each clerk stood at his usual place, all looking as solemn as owls. I went at once into the bank parlor, and there I saw a sight that I never shall forget. I was really alarmed. I dropped into the first chair at hand.

Ebenezer Cook was walking the floor, back and forth, swinging his arms, and tearing his hair out by the handful. Every time he passed me, he gave me such a wild, terrible look that I thought he had gone mad.

He crossed the room in this way ten or twelve times, neither of us saying a word.

I then said: "Cook, what is the matter?"

He stopped in front of me and exclaimed: "I am ruined! you are ruined!—we are all ruined together!"

He went to the table and picked up a dispatch, which he handed to me, saying: "Read that."

It was from George B. Sargent, in Boston. The dispatch said: "If Clarissa will give seventy-five thousand acres"—and something else, which I have forgotten—"we can go on."

Ebenezer Cook stood by me while I read the telegram, and when I handed it back, he said: "If I had received that an hour sooner, I would not have stopped—" He hesitated a minute, and then added, despairingly: "Yes, I would, too. There is some one to be taken care of at this end of the line, as well as at the other."

As there was nothing to be done, I went back to the store, and found it in possession of the sheriff. We had endorsed some one's paper, and the holder sued out an attachment before our own creditors made a move.

There was so much excitement that day that I did not think of the package of county orders I had left in Cook & Sargent's bank the day before.

The next day Prettyman said: "What are we going to do about paying the men?" We had a large number to pay—coopers, mill-men, and clerks.

I replied: "I will get the money to pay them. I have about eight hundred dollars in county orders over at the bank, and will go over and get them and have them cashed."

The morning the bank failed, all the money we had in the world, except our own circula-tion, was a Bank of Florence five-dollar bill. It was so early we had not drawn our usual supply of money for the day's business.

I went over to the bank, and into the bank parlor, where I had left my package of county orders, and looked the place over thoroughly, until I was satisfied that the orders were not there. I was just going out when John P. Cook came in.

He said: "Burrows, what are you looking for?"

I answered: "I am looking for a package of county orders I left here day before yes-terday."

Cook said: "It is not here."

I said: "Yes, it is; I left it lying on the table."

He answered, in a hesitating manner: "Yes; I know you did."

I asked: "Well, where is it, then?"

He replied: "McCosh, the County Treasurer, was down here, crying and howling, and I gave him all ours and yours, too."

"Why," said I, "Mr. Cook, they did not belong to you; you had no business to give McCosh my property to pay your debts."

He answered: "I suppose I had not; but he was making such a noise and fuss that I wanted to quiet him; but I will make it good to you."

He never has made it good to me, and I have no reason to think that he ever will.

Chapter 38

Action at Law Against Cook & Sargent.—The Mortgage on Clifton.—Victory in the Lower Court, but Reversal in the Supreme Tribunal.—The Revelation of After Years.—A Single Judge Casts the Die from Sympathy.—Gross Injustice All Around.

AFTER the failure of Cook & Sargent, not being able to get any satisfaction or protection from them on the twenty-thousand-dollar mortgage to Le Claire, nor to get pay for my county orders, which they took after their failure, I brought suit against them, my attorney, Judge Grant, believing that if I could show that I did not owe Cook & Sargent anything at the time when the mortgage was given, I could get it set aside.

The result of the suit was a judgment in favor of Burrows & Prettyman for one hundred and ten thousand dollars, as the bank books showed that on the day the Le Claire mortgage was given, Cook & Sargent owed Burrows & Prettyman that amount.

This suit was brought on a basis of ten per cent interest from the time we began business with Cook & Sargent until the date of the mortgage. We presented a statement and our bank books to the Supreme Court. Cook & Sargent did not dispute the same, and although we showed that they owed us at the time the mortgage was given, it was of no avail, as, on account of innocent parties interested in the mortgage, it had to stand.

The last time I saw Mr. Lindley, of the law firm of Cook, Dillon & Lindley, was about ten years ago, at the corner of Second and Brady streets.

After shaking hands, Mr. Lindley drew me to one side, and said: "I want to talk with you." We sat down on a dry-goods box, and he said:

"Well, how is the world treating you now-a-days?"

I replied: "Rather roughly."

He asked me what I was doing, and I told him I was farming, gardening, and filibustering around, trying to make a living.

He said: "Burrows, I am sorry for you. Cook & Sargent treated you badly; but, if possible, they treated me worse than they did you, when I came to settle with them. Do you know how near you came to saving your home on the hill?"

I answered: "Well, I can't say that I do."

He continued: "You came devilish near it. You only lost it by one vote in the Supreme Court, and that Judge hesitated a whole year. He hated to take your place from you, and if it had been only Cook & Sargent and you who were interested, you would have saved your place. But George B. Sargent had obtained the money from an estate in Boston, where the money was needed to support and educate orphan children."

Mr. Lindley was a very fine man, and while he was employed on the opposite side in the suit, his sympathies were with me.

Shortly after the dissolution of the law firm of Cook, Dillon & Lindley, which quickly followed the failure of Cook & Sargent, Mr. Lindley went to St. Louis; represented that district in Congress two terms, and then was appointed a judge in one of the St. Louis courts.[32]

The mill and Burrows' block had been placed in the hands of a receiver, and rented to me for five thousand dollars a year.

At the end of the first year the receiver told me: "You are paying too much rent. I am going to get it reduced to twenty-five hundred dollars a year;" and he did.

[32] The author's memory is not entirely accurate at this point. James J. Lindley was a representative in Congress from Missouri from 1853 to 1857. He located in Davenport in 1858, where he practiced law until the close of the Civil War. He then removed to Chicago, and in 1868 to St. Louis, where he became Circuit Court judge. He died at Nevada, Mo., April 18, 1891. See *Biog. Cong. Directory* (Washington, 1913).

Chapter 39

THE failure of Cook & Sargent, at that time, was a great surprise to me, and I think it was unexpected by them. It is my opinion that they had no idea of it the day before; but a bank doing such a business as they always had done, not having three hundred dollars on hand when it closed at three o'clock, showed that there was something rotten somewhere. If Cook & Sargent had not failed, Burrows & Prettyman would have gone safely through the crisis. Our financial situation was much better than it had been. Our circulation was nearly out of the way. A wealthy relative in Norfolk, Virginia, had lent me ten thousand dollars, to assist us in retiring our checks, and would have done more if it had been necessary.

The winter after the failure we were idle, completely tied up. In the spring, Mr. Prettyman accepted a situation as agent of the Northern Line Packet Company, and I arranged to get the management of my mill and Burrows' Block, and was making a com-

fortable living when the Civil War broke out.
The years 1860 and 1861, and a part of 1862,
were unfavorable for milling—1860, very
much so. I had a large lot of flour in New
Orleans, unsold, and communication with
that city was about suspended, and to close
out the flour our agents were compelled to
sell it at auction, causing me a loss.

In the latter part of 1863, prospects improved, and as I expected to do a large fall
business, I laid up my mill for repairs during
harvest. I spent about twenty-five hundred
dollars on it, and had just got it ready to
run when it was destroyed by fire.

The bolts did not work right, and for some
time I had been running nights and laying
still during the day, to overhaul the bolts,
etc. The repairs were to be finished the day
of the fire. This was right in harvest. I used
to raise a good deal of wheat then, and, having about one thousand acres that year, I
was in the habit of going out to the wheat-
fields every day during harvest, after I had
arranged my business in town. I had a contract for flour, and the boat was expected
that day. I told the miller not to shut down
the mill until the shipment was out; then
the millwrights could finish their job. The
flour was not out until about noon, when the
millwrights took possession.

I went out into the country about nine o'clock, came home at noon, ate my dinner, and went immediately to the mill. I found no one there, the men not having returned from dinner. I counted the flour, and found the shipment was out. I had set a man to work, that morning, in the upper story, cleaning out a lot of rubbish, and went up to see what he had done.

As I came down stairs to the third floor, where the bolting-chests were situated, I cast my eyes upward and saw a little whiff of smoke curling around overhead, about as much as a man would puff when smoking a cigar. I stood and looked at it. In a moment it disappeared, and I concluded it was a puff of steam which had found its way from the engine-room.

I walked down stairs, and met a farmer from Pleasant Valley, who was looking for me. He wanted me to send him some harvest hands. After talking with him for ten minutes, I went to the office of the Northern Line Packet Company to see Mr. Pretty-man about some wheat he had in store, which I had bought and wanted delivered at the mill that afternoon, as it was to be ground that night. I found the teamster loading it up, and then went to my own office, No. 2 Burrows' Block. I asked my son, who was clerking for me, what time it was. He looked at his watch, and said it was twenty minutes past two. I said I would write my Chicago letter, and then go to the field. I picked up pen and ink, and had written but two lines when a friend, Oscar A. Barker, familiarly known as "Father Barker," came rushing to the door, and said:

"Mr. Burrows, I believe your mill is on fire."

I rushed out, and the blackest smoke I ever saw was pouring out of the third-story windows, where the bolts the men had been working at were placed.

As I ran up stairs, I saw the engineer, and cried: "The mill is on fire! Give the alarm, and bring water, quick; perhaps we can put it out."

As soon as I reached the head of the stairs I saw that it was too late. I then exclaimed: "Never mind the water; try to get out the flour."

The flour was in the second story. It was too late to save even that. The fire leaped from elevator to elevator, and in five minutes from the time it was discovered, the whole mill, from the cellar to the roof, was a mass of flames.

To the repeated inquiry, "Mr. Burrows, how did your mill get on fire? I answered:

"It must have been set on fire." But at night one of the packers came to my house, and said:

"I have come to tell you how your mill got on fire. Mr. Drew, the millwright, is responsible for it. He had been examining the bolts inside the bolting-chests, using a candle for that purpose, and when he went to dinner, he left the candle burning inside the chest, and closed the doors, so that the light could not be seen. The weather was hot, and the candle burned away rapidly, possibly fell over, and so ignited the bolting-cloths."

The little whiff of smoke I had seen must have found its way through some crack. There was twenty-five thousand dollars insurance on the mill, but it all went to my creditors. My individual loss on stock was about six thousand dollars, and I had no insurance.

Chapter 40

Once More in the Milling Line, and Once More Wiped
Out by Fire.—Close of My Business Career, and
Beginning of Days Darkened by Poverty.—Sketches
of My Two Staunch Business Associates, Robert M.
Prettyman and James E. Woodruff.

IF that mill had not burned, I might have
made up my losses, and been in good
shape again. I had made some money
that summer, and had the means to run the
mill to advantage that fall. It was the largest mill in the State, and made from three
hundred and fifty to five hundred barrels of
flour a day. It made, once, five hundred and
forty barrels in one day. This mill cost me
about sixty thousand dollars, and in a favorable season made money fast; and if I had
had the use of it during the latter part of the
war, from 1863 to 1865, it would have
brought me out all right again. As George
Hawley, of Pleasant Valley, said to me once,
a man could not help making money during
the war. He said:

"You could not turn over a stone without
finding a greenback under it."

After a brief period of inactivity, I decided to try milling once more, and bought

the lot at Fifth and Harrison streets, where there had been an elevator, which had been burned. I also bought a small mill at Atalissa, and brought it in and put it up on the lot, but labored under many disadvantages. I spent about fifteen hundred dollars trying to get a supply of water, but failed. Sometimes I had to hire teams to haul water from the river; sometimes, also, to catch water as it ran down the gutters, which damaged the boilers, causing constant expense; but, notwithstanding all this, the mill had nearly paid for itself, when another fire occurred, and Mill No. 2 was burned down.

This mill, like the other, had been laid up for repairs, and was nearly ready for business when it took fire from spontaneous combustion, caused by a pile of slack coal in the engine-room. The building was entirely destroyed.

This ended my efforts in the milling line, as I did not have the means to continue, and could not see much inducement to erect another mill; and so I turned my attention to farming and gardening, which I found a hard way to earn a living; but I persevered until a year ago, when my health broke down, and since then I have been shelved.

Before closing these reminiscences of business ventures and vicissitudes, I desire to record here, as humble tributes to their memories, brief sketches of the two men nearest to me as business associates during my career, and both dead before me.

Robert M. Prettyman, so long my partner, and so close to me, not only in business life, but personal relations, died in Davenport, from cholera, on September 3, 1873, while acting as agent for the Northern Line Packet Company, the position that I have already said he accepted on retiring from the firm of Burrows & Prettyman. Mr. Prettyman was generous, hospitable, and courteous, extremely popular among his associates, and respected by all who knew him. He was born in Sussex County, Delaware, on July 5, 1813; being the only son, and youngest of three children, of Isaac and Hannah Prettyman. His mother died in Sussex, when Robert was only four years old, and his father died six years later. After the death of his father, Robert lived with his grandmother until he was seventeen years old, when she apprenticed him to a dry-goods merchant, with whom he remained until he was twenty-one years old. He then emigrated, first to Illinois, where he worked at farming for a short time, and thence, not liking agriculture, to Davenport, in 1840. He first found a situation as clerk in a hotel, but soon gave it up to begin as clerk, and afterwards to become a partner in the firm of Burrows & Prettyman, as chronicled in the foregoing record. Mr. Prettyman was married to Julia H. Logue, on August 14, 1843, in Davenport. He left two children, a daughter and son—Mrs. A. Kimball and Robert M. Prettyman.

I have mentioned the name of James E. Woodruff in this book, repeatedly, as having been my best business friend, and one to whose kindness and generosity I attribute, in a great measure, such business successes as at times I scored. He was a noble man, generous, high-minded, and indefatigable in his business. No merchant stood higher in business circles in St. Louis or New York than he. His close attention to business affected his health, and in 1855, the year after I had consulted him about the Crimean War wheat speculations, his physician said that he was threatened with softening of the brain, and recommended that he take a trip to Europe.[33] Mr. Woodruff had a brother-

[33] The author's memory is faulty at this point. This voyage was evidently made in 1854, since the *Arctic*, on which Woodruff was returning home, was wrecked in September of this year. See *post*, Note 34.

in-law, E. K. Collins, a rich Quaker, of New
York City, who was the owner of the famous
Collins line of ocean steamships, consisting
of four first-class vessels, running from New
York to Liverpool, one of which made the
quickest trip ever made across the Atlantic
up to that time. It became the favorite line,
but did not exist long. Two of the vessels
being lost within ten years, the enterprise
was abandoned. The lost vessels were the
Pacific and the *Arctic*. Mr. Woodruff had
passed three or four months abroad, and,
with improved health, was returning with
his family, on the *Arctic*, when, during a
heavy fog, off Cape Race, she was run into
by some other vessel, and so badly damaged
that she sank with nearly all on board. A
gentleman, one of the few saved, brought the
report that the Captain, after examining
into the damage done to the boat, informed
the passengers that there was no hope; they
must go down. The boat was sinking inch
by inch; and just before the final lurch, Mr.
Woodruff was seen standing on deck, perfectly calm, his wife clinging to one hand
and his daughters to the other. He held them
close, and seemed to be trying to comfort
them, when the vessel shuddered and
plunged violently, and in an instant disap-

peared forever. Nothing more was ever
heard of James E. Woodruff.[34]

[34] The steamer *Arctic* of the Collins Line, enroute
from Liverpool to New York, collided with the French
steamer *Vesta*, off Cape Race, Sept. 21, 1854. The
Vesta made the port of St. Johns, while the *Arctic* sank
with the loss of almost all the passengers and crew,
about 370 in number. The disaster created a marked
impression upon the public mind, owing in part to the
attendant circumstances of the sinking and in part to
the prominence of many of the victims, among whom
were numbered the wife, son, and daughter of Mr.
Collins. See *Annual Register . . . of the year 1854*
(London, 1855), "Chronicle," p. 161–63.

Chapter 41[35]

A Closing Retrospection.

THE changes fifty years produce no one can realize, unless he has experienced them. When my mind reverts to the scenes of 1838, and my memory calls up the struggles and poverty of the pioneer settlers the first ten years of my residence in Scott County, and then considers what those men and women accomplished with their iron nerve, their tireless energy, their large hearts and strong arms, my heart is filled with joy and pride that I am reckoned one of them.

When I see the results of those early struggles, I do not regret, even now—when, after fifty years of exertion, I am overtaken with old age, ill-health, and poverty—that I cast my lot and united my efforts with those brave pioneers in laying the foundation of what we are all proud of—the beautiful City of Davenport, and the banner county of the State of Iowa, Old Scott!

[35] In the original edition this final chapter is Chapter XLII. It is here renumbered, since we omit to reprint the author's story of the founding of Oakdale Cemetery, constituting his original Chapter XLI.

And while, financially, I am even worse off than when I landed here, on the bright 27th day of July, 1838, I flatter myself that I have contributed something toward the sum total of prosperity that now smiles upon the scene which was then practically unsettled, unimproved, and almost unknown.

Fifty years ago, Davenport contained only about twenty-five dwelling-houses, and a scant one hundred and fifty inhabitants. The western part of town, below what is now called Ripley Street, was a mere swamp, where neither man nor beast could venture without danger of miring. Repeatedly has the writer assisted in rescuing cattle and horses from the quagmire that existed there, prying up with boards, and dragging out with ropes, the live stock of our neighbors. Now, that dangerous bog is covered with substantial brick dwellings and paved streets; the little village of one hundred and fifty inhabitants has grown to a beautiful city of thirty thousand; and more houses are erected now in one year than the pioneers, struggling with poverty, were able to build the first ten years.

Fifty years ago, our dwellings and business houses were small one and one-half story frame buildings; now, the new court-house, the Masonic Temple, the Turner Hall, and the substantial business houses erected in recent years, are a source of pride to what few old settlers are left.

Fifty years ago, our church-going people worshiped in warehouses, carpenter-shops, or any rooms they could find vacant. School-houses, we had none. Now, our church-buildings and our school-houses are a credit to the State.

Fifty years ago, Scott County did not raise enough provisions to feed the few hundred inhabitants. Now, Scott County stands No. 1 in her business and her productions.

Fifty years ago, we had, comparatively speaking, no money. Many a pioneer could not raise the twenty-five cents with which to pay the postage on the letter from the dear ones he had left at his old home. Now, Scott County is the wealthiest county in the State of Iowa, and the bulk of her wealth is the savings of honest labor, the fruit of the planting of fifty years ago.

Truly, the wilderness has blossomed as the rose. The seed planted by the pioneer, taking quick root, has transformed the lonely prairies into magnificent farms. The small cluster of houses at the foot of Ripley Street has grown until it covers an area of three miles east and west, and one and one-half miles north and south.

I had occasion to go into the Masonic Temple a few days before writing these lines, and as I viewed its beauty, extent, and facilities for convenience, my thoughts went back to 1838, and I remembered the many Saturday nights, I had waited until nine or ten o'clock, in the little twelve-by-fourteen post-office which stood on the same ground, for our eastern mail, which we received only every other Saturday night.

When I gaze upon Davenport's new and magnificent court-house, and consider the large amount of books and stationery now used for county purposes, I think of the first two years of my business in the town (1840–41), when Ebenezer Cook was County Clerk, and I used to bring, twice a year, from Cincinnati, in my trunk, all the books and stationery needed.

But, while I notice with joy and pride these great changes in the progress and wealth of Scott County, Oakdale, the city of the dead, suggests other thoughts.

In looking over my books and papers, containing the records of transactions forty to fifty years ago, I am filled with sadness as I read over the names of those with whom I was associated so intimately, and find so few of them still living. I cannot recall more than twenty persons alive in Scott County, as I write, who were here when I came here, in 1838. And we few that are left must soon go to join those that have rested from their labors, and the time is near at hand when it will be said:

"The last Old Settler is gone."

Index

303

Index

Bears, killed, 10–11.

Beer, Civil War promotes drinking, 140.

Bellevue, site of Fox village, 29.

Black Buffalo, gives information, 47–48; horse deserts, 57; slain, 65–66

Black Hawk, patriotism, XVII; wigwam appropriated, 15, 23–25; rivalry with Keokuk, 26–27, 77–80; condemns whisky, 27–28; opposes Treaty of 1804, 37, 43–44; ancestry, 38; driven from Rock Island, 40–50; policy of nonviolence, 44, 49–50; defeats Major Stillman, 55–57; peace proffers rebuffed, 56, 72; captured, 75; eastern tour, 76–77; closing years, 77–80; burial, 80; body stolen, 81. See also Indians, Black Hawk War, and Sauk and Foxes.

Black Hawk War, Spencer describes, XVII–XVIII; causes, 36–50; events described, 50–79.

Bliss, Major John, action against Black Hawk, 47–48.

Bloomington, predecessor of Muscatine, 115.

Bluffdale, early settlement, 9.

Brasher, Wm. T., pioneer settler, 23.

Brazil, early steamboat, 105–106, 108.

Brimstone Corner, 126.

British Party, Black Hawk leads, 38.

Buffalo Grove, attacked, 60.

Burials, Indian, 80–82; in early Davenport, 127.

Burlington, early steamboat, 118.

Burnell, Strong, breaks prairie, 113.

Burrows' Block, built, 261; rented, 286; office in, 289.

Burrows, David A., removal to Iowa, 120; perpetrates hoax, 128–30; peddles vegetables, 136–137.

Burrows, John A. D., Cincinnati merchant, 137; nobility of, 141.

Burrows, John M. D., narrative characterized, XVIII–XIX; reasons for writing, 93–96; migration to Davenport, 105–21; journey from Cincinnati to Davenport, 108–10; purchases land, 112–13; river journey to St. Louis, 114–19; loses money, 116, 157,

304

Index

Index

Index

Index

Index

Index

Minnesota Territory, organized, XVI.

Mississippi River, crossed, 9, 47, 50, 78, 106–107; Campbell's expedition, 11–14; journeys via, 17–20, 105–106, 108, 114–20, 154–61, 168–69, 176–80, 182–85, 245–49; Indians retreat to, 70; Bad Axe battle, 72–75; early closing, 205; canal planned, 206; Zachary Taylor's expedition, 219; activities of Edward Davidson, 228–30.

Mississippi Valley, white settlement, XV–XVI.

Missouri, settlers leave, 9–11; boundary dispute, 121–24.

Missouri War, described, 121–24.

Muscatine, early history, 115; Burrows visits, 170–71, 178–79; hog-packing center, 233–35.

NAHPOPE, in Black Hawk War, 57–59, 72; prisoner, 76.

Nauvoo, history, 117; relations with Prophet Smith, 180.

Nauvoo, steamboat, 180.

Nelson, Capt. Joseph S., commandant of Fort Armstrong, 25.

Newburg, predecessor of Muscatine, 115.

Newcomb, Daniel T., relations with, 170–74.

Newcomb, Mrs. Daniel T., characterized, 173–74.

New Orleans, market center, 175–76, 182–85, 288.

Newspapers, established, 128–30; wage bank war, 250–52, 273.

Nicholas, czar of Russia, effects of death, 269–70.

Noncombatants, Black Hawk in rôle of, 44, 49–50; slain, 71, 73–75.

OAKDALE Cemetery, established, 128.

Owens, John, career, 108; migration to Iowa, 108–13; return journey, 114–19.

Owens, Mrs. John, as neighbor, 145.

PASHPAHAW, prisoner, 76.

Payne, Rev. Adam, slain, 68–69.

Pecatonica, battle, 61–62.

Pence, Judge ——, early settler, 15, 17, 25.

311

Index

Perry, ———, early settler, 172; land sold, 215.

Pierce, ———, early settler, 19–20.

Pig's Eye, early name for St. Paul, 153.

Pike, Benj. J., elected Ranger captain, 44.

Pleasant Valley, early settlers listed, 110–11.

Plum River, early settlers, 17; visited, 18–20.

Pork. See Hogs.

Potosi. See Snake Hollow.

Potatoes, hoax related, 128–30; speculation in, 182–85.

Prairie du Chien, military operations at, 11–13; visits to, 150–51, 154–61.

Prairies, beauty, 109–10; broken, 113.

Presbyterian Church, founded, 125; story of Rev. Michael Hummer, 131–35.

Prettyman, Robt. M., employee of Burrows, 150–52, 167, 179–80; partner, 181–82, 189–90, 225–28, 273, 276, 282; cashes bank notes, 236; steamship agent, 287, 289, 294; career, 294–95. See also John M. D. Burrows and Burrows and Prettyman.

Princeton, site of Fox village, 15.

Prince, ———, early settler, 15.

Quashquama (Jumping Fish), negotiates treaty, 46.

Railroads, travel conditions on, 119; built, 152–53, 264.

Reynolds, Gov. Thomas, in Black Hawk War, 41–50, 55–57.

Roads, described, 109.

Rockingham War, described, 121–22, 139.

Rockingham Mill, operations, 186–89, 194–95, 208.

Rock Island, natural advantages, XV; early settlers, 14–17, 23; Sauk and Fox Indians described, 15–16, 20–39, 81–82; expelled, 40–50; reception of Black Hawk, 77–80.

Rock Island City, named, 105.

Rock Island County, organized, 105.

Rock Island House, 106.

Rock River, Indian hostilities on, 40–59, 70. See also Indians and Sauk and Fox Indians.

Index

313

Index

Snyder, Capt. Adam, leader in Indian fight, 68.

Spanish dollar, use of, 155–56.

Spencer, John W., narrative characterized, XVII–XVIII; printed, 5–85; reasons for writing, 5–7; migration to Missouri, 9; to Illinois, 10–11; removal to Rock Island, 15–23; carries mail, 17–20; describes Sauk and Fox Indians, 15–16, 20–37, 81–82; relations with Black Hawk, 27–28, 77; militia officer, 44; in Black Hawk War, 47–55; tribute to pioneers, 84–85.

Spencer, R. H., in Kellogg's Grove battle, 67.

Sprague, A. W., and Co., merchants, 141–42.

Squashes, Indians raise, 25.

Squatters, claims explained, 112.

Stagecoaches, travel by, 221–24; boot described, 221–22; missed, 155–57.

Stabbing Chief, prisoner, 76.

Steamboats, at Chicago, XVI; Indian name for, 13–14; Indians ignore, 46–47; on Wisconsin River, 154–55; John Atchison operates, 164–68; Joseph Smith, 180; Burrows, 245–49; Collins Line, 190–91, 296; on Illinois River, 220; wrecked, 268, 296–97.

Stephenson, predecessor of Rock Island City, 105, 110.

Stillman's Run, battle, 55–57.

Suckers, Illinoisans named, 14.

Taylor, Major Zachary, Credit Island defeat, 13, 218–19; in Black Hawk War, 54.

Tillson, Mrs. Christiana H., narrative, 9.

Treaties, with Sauk and Foxes, 36–37, 43–44, 46, 50.

Turner, Dr., steals body of Black Hawk, 81.

Vandruff, Joshua, early settler, 23; Indians threaten, 40.

Vandruff's Island, artillery shells, 48.

Van Tuyl, Wm., early settler, 179; manages flour mill, 186.

Wells, Joel, early settler, 23.

Wells, Rinnah, early settler, 14, 23; quarrel with Indians, 25–27, 40; son slain, 62.

314

Index